FOLKTALES
as
THERAPY

FOLKTALES
as
THERAPY

by
Verena Kast

Translated by Douglas Whitcher

Fromm International
Publishing Corporation
New York

Originally published in 1986 as Märchen als Therapie
Copyright © 1986 Walter-Verlag AG, Olten, Switzerland

Manufactured in the United States of America
Printed on acid-free, recycled paper

First U.S. Edition
Kast, Verena, 1943-
    [Märchen als Therapie, English]
    Folktales as therapy / by Verena Kast : translated from the German by
Douglas Whitcher. — 1st U.S. ed.
        p.   cm
    Translation of: Märchen als Therapie.
    ISBN 0-88064-209-2 — ISBN 0-88064-210-6 (pbk)
    1. Fairy tales—Therapeutic use. 2. Fairy tales—Psychological aspects. I Title.
RC489.F3K3713   1995
616.89'16—dc20   94-30940
                                                                      CIP

CONTENTS

FOREWORD

The folktale intepretations published in this book were originally
delivered as lectures at the Lindauer Psychotherapy Week of 1985
under the title "The Meaning of Folktales in the Therapeutic Process." A somewhat expanded version of these lectures was then
delivered at Zurich University in the summer semester of 1985, and
subsequently published in German by Walter-Verlag.

Here I would like to express my gratitude for all of the generous
and encouraging interest that these thoughts have met with thus
far, as well as for the many suggestions—not all of which I was able
to incorporate.

Most especially, I would like to thank those individuals who
have allowed me not only to relate the necessary details of their life
histories, but also to publish the creative writing that they produced
while working with folktales. They have given me a precious gift.

St. Gallen, August 1985   Verena Kast

INTRODUCTION

Parents, siblings, friends, lovers, and children are not the only ones who play their parts in our biographies; so do stories. Most of us have our favorite tales that we have either heard or read. And most of us have been fascinated time again by one particular tale.

It is not so hard to see that the stories that once captivated us—or still keep their hold on us—tell about who we are, about our longings and wishes. They bring us closer to attitudes and ideals that we would like to call our own, and help us envision the persons we would like to be. But what may be less obvious is that these tales also contain messages about our problems. Like the persons we encounter in our dreams, the characters we remember from folktales often embody issues of pressing personal concern. But these characters not only bring us face to face with our concerns; they often show us a way to deal with them as well.

Folktales accompany us through life; some of us give the impression that our tales are more real than our lives. Beginning at a very early age, we make folktales part of our lives. The folktale is a story, but not just any kind of story. Many things happen in a folktale that are marvelous, twists of fate that we would never in our wildest imagination expect in our actual lives. "Fantastic," we say, "unbelievable, incredible . . . !" At times—if secretly—we would be glad if reality would loosen its wrenching grip on us a bit; we would love to let ourselves be carried along by a belief in "marvelous" solutions, a faith in answers that "we never dreamed of," a hope that creative solutions will dawn on us just when we're giving up. By identifying with the folktale's protagonist, we are imbued with the hope that problems do indeed have solutions, that creative change can never be completely ruled out. In this way the folktale conveys the "courage to be" that can help us get free of the tangles of the past in order to move on more decisively into the uncertain future.

No, the folktale is "not just any kind of story." Not only because it is marvelously hopeful, but also because it has a long oral history. In the course of being handed down, details that are unique to particular storytellers drop away. The end product is a tale stripped down to themes that are of interest to the widest variety of listeners, although literary collectors of folktales, such as the Brothers Grimm, have colored their slightly reworked tales with their own convictions and beliefs.[1]

Structurally, folktales typically begin with a problematic situation.[2] Then they show how the situation might be dealt with. Here is the "way" that must be suffered through; there can be no exemption for the protagonist, whose deeds illustrate a process of emotional growth, whose attitude shows what it will take to face up to the dilemma, and whose way of personal development leads through and out of the problem with which the tale began. These dilemmas are typically human, perhaps universal, which means that the protagonist's trials and tribulations can usually be compared with our own without too much exaggeration.

Folktales, which are closely related to myths, dreams, and unconscious processes in general,[3] speak to us in symbols and images. The elements of their narrative structures correspond to the stages and phases of psychological growth. Encoded in a symbolic language, framed in a cosmic vision, myths pose perennial human questions and provide some keys for answering them as well, although there always remains something that can not be explained in "so many words." Although at times myths express the self-

perception of a particular group, their symbols not only signify
things already known, or things that need to be remembered; they
also steer us toward what we have not yet fully attained. The
mythic symbol thus forms a bridge between immanence and transcendence, and forms a link between the "minute particulars" and
the "sum of all the parts."

Folktales are mythic in some ways, but the symbols that we
encounter in folktales are usually closer to our immediate experience than are those of myths. They speak to the banal and idiosyncratic events of our lives—without losing sight of the "human, too"
aspect of our personal concerns. They show us roads that can take
us to the mines of "things we have yet to discover." It is within this
ground of being that we find the resources that will help us through
our trials.

The symbol combines experiences, psychic contents—and especially emotions—into a sum total that cannot be represented with a
letter, number, or any other sign. Bloch calls the symbol a "category
of condensation." The work of interpreting a symbol never reaches
any final conclusion; since it is "overdetermined" and has a surplus
of meaning, each attempt brings only a bit of the gold to consciousness. It opens up perspectives that gradually yield their riches the
deeper we dig. Yet after all is said and done, there still remains
plenty to be said.

In the depth-psychological interpretation of folktales, where narrative events are viewed side by side with life-span issues of emotional growth, we draw on many of the same techniques that we
use to interpret dreams. "Interpretation on the subjective level," for
example, is a powerful tool that helps us look at the entire cast of
characters as subpersonalities of the protagonist. When a man
meets a witch, we say that he is faced with a witchlike part of himself. By experimentally taking each of the characters in turn as the
protagonist, we generate a number of complementary interpretive
possibilities.[4]

Blazing forth their meaning from many angles, folktale symbols

tend not to weary the mind. Any interpretation that is true illumi-
nates and reveals. No interpretation possesses the sole truth, but if
it is self-consistent and makes sense out of the narrative's most
important features, it contains truth. This is a playful way of interpreting, a game—in the best sense of the word—of reflecting on
life, probing, and plunging into psychic processes.

In working with folktales in therapy, it is important to identify
the primary concern that is unique to each folktale. This will help
us decide which of the many possible methods of interpretation
prove the most fruitful. I will offer this kind of thematic synopsis
for each of the tales to be treated in this book.

In therapy, we try to create an environment in which the tale can
speak to us at the level of the imagination. Many of our inner
images have become hardened and stereotyped. When they are
softened in a therapeutic environment and become accessible to the
folktale's input, there is a chance that our prejudices and fixations
may undergo some alteration. Maybe the power of fantasy can even
be revived. Through the funnel of the inner image, the folktale can
profoundly affect our emotional chemistry. Just listening to a folktale is already therapeutic; if we are receptive, the story's image
"works on us." Granted, some motifs may strike us with greater
immediacy than others. These motifs are quickly offered a room in
our minds. We become their proud and possessive owners, because
they seem to express how we feel in a way that nothing else can.
For instance, we may be paralyzed by a feeling of emptiness and
apathy. We can find no way to express this feeling, nor do we feel
any pressing desire to do so. The symbol of a folktale may lend its
voice.

A woman attempts to describe how she feels. Suddenly it occurs
to her, "I feel like the princess under the thornbush: sleepy and
incredibly prickly on the outside." This folktale image allowed her
to become more articulate about her feeling of being in a deadlock,
about her destructive rage. Soon she was able to imagine how her
emotional state might affect those around her.

Unlike some feelings, the image is something we can look at. In some respects the image belongs to "me." But then again, it is a resource that is independent of me. After all, it is a text. This paradox often provides us with the distance necessary to deal with the problem expressed in the image. The image of the princess in the thornbush belongs to a "magical" type of tale whose narrative structure takes a conflict to a creative conclusion. Therapeutic work with folktales depends on this narrative process. We take our own images and "enter" them into a developmental "program" that is encoded with the hope—characteristic of folktales—that difficulties can be overcome. According to Bloch, every living symbol—every symbol that speaks to us—contains "archetypally encapsulated hope."[5] Surely therapy should be about the business of making available this resource within the human psyche.

There are a number of ways of working with folktales in psychotherapy. We can work with the stories that have always been a part of our lives, that connect us with our childhood and biography. We can use them to confront issues stemming from childhood, and see if they offer any suggestions for how to deal with them. Or we can use the folktale as a mirror to examine our present dilemmas. Then again, we can use the folktale as a means of stimulating a creative process of symbolization, a kind of "imagination" guided by the folktale. This book contains examples of all three ways of working with folktales.

Symbols from folktales provide a forward thrust by dislodging the blocks to emotional development. Working with them allows us to hope. By seeing our personal concerns in the mirror of this extended narrative cosmos, we are reintegrated into a community that shares a belief in solutions.

FOLKTALES
as
THERAPY

LITTLE RED CAP

Favorite and Dreaded Folktales
from Childhood

In a book about the folktales that were our favorites as children, Hans Dieckmann proposed that these stories describe our primary complexes and the typical ways that we learn to behave in relation to them. Dieckmann described a neurotic person as someone who has not completed the tasks prescribed for the folktale's hero. This could be someone who has failed to live up to a heroic quest, but it could also be someone who lives in unconscious, literal imitation of the hero's quest.[6]

If Dieckmann's thesis is correct, then both the tales that we most wanted to hear as children and those that we were most frightened by give us information about the main constellations of complexes that have more or less ruled our lives. But this thesis requires a distinction between those persons who had only one favorite story from childhood and others who can think of several different tales that were important at different stages of their lives. Then there is the question of whether these various tales actually describe one underlying issue. But even if this variety of stories deals with one basic theme, the variety suggests a personality that has not gotten caught in one way of dealing with everything, but rather has developed a repertoire of responses. There would be a greater degree of freedom within the restrictions that a complex constellation always poses.[7]

To make something of our favorite childhood tales in therapy, the analysand needs to adopt the attitude of the the hero or heroine, according to Dieckmann, and thus profit from the completion of tasks that takes place in the story. Then this identification with the tale's protagonist needs to be dissolved again. In the case of tales in which the hero is doomed to failure, the analysand would have to take on the hero's fate in such a way that the defeat that seems to be prescribed can be avoided.

By working with our favorite tales, we can identify the structure of complexes that is at the basis of our problems. From my experience, I would modify Dieckmann's thesis. I have seldom met anyone whose entire structure of complexes was expressed in a single tale that they recalled from their childhood. But I agree that one fundamental problem does come to expression there: Rather than remembering the tale first, I have the impression that we often recall a particular tale once we have identified a certain structure of complexes. Moreover, until this structure has been identified, it is generally premature to begin working with folktales.

One difficulty in working with favorite tales of childhood is that they are often quite difficult to recall. To aid the memory, it sometimes helps to think of costumes that we liked to wear when we were children, typical drawings, storybooks—especially those pages that seem to have been more frequently referred to than others.

Often favorite childhood stories are recalled by associating to dreams that arise in therapy. Naturally, the attitude of the therapist greatly influences such matters. Is he or she likely to notice folktale motifs in dreams? Does this sort of work appeal to him or her?

Clinical Illustration
    A 38-year-old woman has been through 150 hours of an analysis as part of her training. The incentive to work with folktales

came from a short series of dreams: "I am dreaming of wolves that needed to be fed. I wake up. In the twilight between dreaming and waking I think, 'I am traveling on a lonely road.'"

Before beginning the work of gathering associations, I responded with the suggestion, "Try taking a look at the story of Little Red Cap." She looked at me in surprise, and told me that Little Red Cap had been a very important story for her when she was little. What had most captivated her about the tale was the idea of "straying from the path." Her face shone as she told me this. She insisted that she still really liked that part of the story. At Fasnacht (carnival) time, she had often dressed up as Little Red Cap. And once when she saw her mother snoring with her mouth wide open, she was startled by the thought that her mother was the wolf in disguise.

My intervention had unearthed a favorite folktale from childhood. At this point I invited my analysand to "play with" the tale. Of course, just because she dreamed of a wolf did not mean that she saw herself as Little Red Cap; this story has no monopoly on wolves. So what made me think of Little Red Cap? I believe it is safe to say that here was an incidence of syntonic countertransference. That is, I intuitively introduced symbolic material into the therapeutic process that gave expression to the analysand's unconscious problem. I define "syntonic countertransference" as the perception and verbalization of a feeling that the analyst has in connection with a feeling or unconscious constellation of the analysand. This particular countertransference image arose in part out of my knowledge of the analysand's constellation of complexes, in part out of her present problem, and in part from the association she made to her dream between the wolf and loneliness. However, despite attempts to account for countertransference in this manner, there is always something else in such interventions that cannot adequately be accounted for.

The analysand comes from a family in which there were no clear boundaries between the generations. A child of her father's second marriage, she had brothers who were old enough to be her father. Her father died when she was four years old. The most dependable and important person in her life was her mother. Her relationship with her mother continued to be very important and strong. Patient and good-natured, her mother represented the one stable factor in a family that was otherwise very turbulent. The analysand—I shall call her Angela—had an intense anxiety-aggression problem that had become especially acute, since she had just begun a new job. In the past she had done odd jobs requiring no special qualifications. Later she went back to school and on to university studies, after which she got a good job. Although she had done well in her studies, she was often intensely afraid of exposing herself to embarrassment, especially in groups, when her entire body trembled, especially her neck and throat.

She was open to therapeutic work on her anxiety, but until now we had not dealt directly with the energy that I saw expressed in the wolf of the Little Red Cap story. She was not able to be assertive in many situations that required it. She was afraid, as it were, of the wolf and of the aggression that she had delegated to the wolf.

A countertransference response that takes the form of such symbolic material is of course possible only among therapists who are familiar with folk literature and have some acquaintance with the realm of meaning to which they belong and the basic issues they address.

Analysts thus have something to gain by learning about the interpretation of folktales. Not that therapy would ever consist of a literal interpretation of fairy tales as such; what usually takes place in therapy is a close examination of the analysand's life and experience in relation to a specific motif. Something unique takes place when a folktale is introduced into the therapeutic situation: attention is shifted slightly from its narrow focus on the relationship between analyst and analysand. They now share a concern with the folktale and its relation to the analysand's life. Expectations are also laid upon the folktale—rather than on the therapist alone—to give courage and suggest strategies for coping with one's problems. Steps are taken toward independence from the therapist. On the other hand, if the therapist introduces a tale at a less advantageous moment, the analysand will not typically be distracted for long.

THE STORY[8]

Once there was a sweet young girl. Everyone who set eyes on her liked her, most of all her grandmother, who wanted to give her something but couldn't decide what. Finally she gave her a little cap made of red velvet. She looked so good in it and was so fond of it that she never took it off. So everyone called her Little Red Cap.

One day her mother said to her, "Come, Little Red Cap, take this bottle of wine and these cakes to your grandmother. She is sick and tired, and they will do her good. Now be a good little girl and give her my greetings. Keep your mind on where you're going and don't stray from the path, otherwise you might fall and break the bottle and your poor grandmother would have nothing." Little Red Cap gave her mother her word—"I will do everything just as you say."

Her grandmother lived in a house deep in the woods a half an hour away from the village. At the edge of the forest Little Red Cap met the wolf. Having no idea what a bad animal he was, she wasn't the least bit afraid of him. "Hello, Little Red Cap," he said. "Oh, hello, wolf." "Where are you going so early in the day?" "To see my grandmother." "What is that you are carrying in your apron?" "Wine and cakes for my grandmother, who is sick and tired. We baked them yesterday to make her feel better." "Little Red Cap, where does your grandmother live?" "If you keep going another quarter of an hour or so into the forest, you can see her house there beneath the three oak trees. Then come the nut hedges. But you know that," said Little Red Cap. "This young and tender thing," thought the wolf to himself, "what a nice, juicy morsel for me. How shall I move in on my prey?" He walked along beside her for a while, and then said, "Little Red Cap, don't you see all the beautiful forest flowers? Have a look! You are missing the lovely birdsong. You are walking as if you were late for school. You could be enjoying the wonder of the forest."

Little Red Cap opened her eyes. When she noticed the sun dancing back and forth through the trees and the beautiful flowers all in bloom, she thought, "Grandma will certainly be pleased if I bring her a bouquet too. It's still early. I don't have to worry about being late." So she jumped off the path into the forest and began gathering flowers there. As soon as she had picked one, she thought she saw another that was even more beautiful, so she went to get it, making her way deeper and deeper into the forest. Meanwhile, the wolf went straight to her grandmother's house and knocked on the door. "Who's there?" "It's me, Little Red Cap. I brought you some pie and wine. Open the door." "Just press down on the handle; I'm too weak to get up." The wolf pressed on the handle, and without a word went right to her bed and swallowed her whole. Then he undressed her and put on her clothes, placed her bonnet on his head, got into her bed, and drew the curtains closed.

Little Red Cap was busy running about gathering flowers. When she had as many as she could carry, she suddenly thought of her grandmother again and made straight for her house without delaying any longer. The door was ajar when she arrived, which made her wonder. When she entered the living room, everything looked slightly out of place. "I don't like it," she thought to herself. "I feel so uneasy today for some reason. Usually I am glad to be here." She went to her grandmother's bed and drew back the curtains. There was her grandmother lying there. She looked strange with the bonnet pulled down so far over her face. "Your ears are so big, Grandma!" "That helps me to hear you better." "And your eyes are so large, Grandma." "That helps me see you better." "But your hands are so big, Grandma." "That helps me to grab you better." "You have such a horribly large mouth, Grandma." "That helps me to eat you better." No sooner said than done—the wolf hopped out of bed, went straight for Little Red Cap, and gobbled her up.

Once the wolf had consumed his delicious meal, he lay down in bed, fell asleep, and began to snore more loudly than he should.

Just then a hunter was passing by. "Can an old lady snore like that?" thought the hunter. "I think I had better take a look and make sure everything is O.K." When he entered the living room and came to the bed, there was the wolf lying in it, the same wolf he had been tracking for quite some time. He was about to shoot the wolf when it occurred to him that he might have devoured the grandmother, whom he might still be able to rescue. So instead of shooting, he took a pair of scissors and snipped open the sleeping wolf's belly. After making a couple of snips, he saw the cheery glow of Little Red's cap. After a few more snips, the girl jumped out. "I was so scared in that wolf's belly; it was so dark!" And then the grandmother came out alive as well. Little Red Cap went right away and got some heavy stones to fill up the wolf's empty belly. When he woke up he wanted to run away, but the stones were so heavy that he collapsed immediately and fell down dead on the spot.

All three enjoyed themselves: the hunter got the wolf's skin, the grandmother ate the cakes and drank the wine that Red Cap had brought her, and Red Cap gave herself a good talking-to: "Never again are you going to stray from the path and go off alone into that forest if your mother forbids it!"

It is also told that when Little Red Cap went to bring her old grandma the cakes again, another wolf spoke to her in the attempt to lead her astray. But Little Red Cap was on her guard and continued straight on and reported to her grandmother that she had seen the wolf, who had wished her a good day and had given her a nasty look. "If I hadn't been on the main road, he would have swallowed me up. We'd better close the doors so he can't get in," she warned. Soon the wolf came knocking. "Open up, Grandma, it's me, Little Red Cap. I've got some baked goods for you." They kept quiet and didn't open the door. The evil one circled around the house a few times before he jumped up onto the roof with the idea of waiting until Little Red Cap went home at night. His idea was to follow her and devour her in the dark of the night. But Grandmother knew what he was thinking. In front of the house there was a stone trough. "Go and fetch the kettle, Little Red

Cap," Grandmother instructed the child. "I cooked sausages in it yesterday. Pour the water from the kettle into the trough." So Little Red Cap filled up the huge stone trough with water from the kettle by the hearth. When the wonderful odor of the sausages entered the wolf's nostrils, he sniffed and looked down. He stuck his neck out so far that he lost his balance and started to slip. He slid down from the roof, fell right into the big trough, and drowned. Red Cap went home feeling pleased. After that, the wolf never did anyone any harm.

When we look at folktales that were important for us as children, it is always worth comparing what we remember with the tale as actually written. Of course, there is usually more than one version of any given tale. Often we have worked out our own version of the tale, and this idiosyncratic version says a lot about our experiences in childhood. When we go back and read these folktales again, we can get more out of them if we concentrate on their images. Priority should be given to those images that had a particular effect on us. Then we profit most from what is unique about folktales: namely, their ability to speak to us on the level of images and feelings.[9]

PERSPECTIVES AND LEVELS OF INTERPRETATION

The story of Little Red Cap is extremely well known, and continues to be the subject of countless parodies, new versions, and films. Little Red Cap has emancipated herself in the process of gaining all this attention. For instance, she rarely allows herself to be devoured anymore. Entire books have been written about "Little Red Riding Hood," as well as an endless variety of interpretive essays.[10] It would seem impossible to do without Little Red Cap. Most children have been affected by the story at some time in their lives, and it seems still to have an effect on adults as well. When people are asked what their favorite or most-feared story was in childhood, Little Red

Cap is mentioned again and again.[11] It is typically cited as a favorite tale when one's memory of it ends with the forest; one identifies with the Little Red Cap who strays from the straight and narrow path in order to discover the wonderful flowers (as with Angela). It is typically cited as the most-feared tale when what one remembers is the business of being devoured and enclosed within the darkness of the wolf's belly.

The overabundance of interpretive essays may be explained by the fact that so many people have been exposed to the tale. Or perhaps it is because the tale is so opaque in so many places. In any case, no definitive interpretation exists. Nor will I be able to offer the most elegant interpretation. Specialists of folk literature such as Scherf[12] do not automatically classify the tale as a magical tale because it is lacking the transformation that would put it in that category. "Little Red Cap" may well be a very primitive tale, pasted together without much aesthetic consideration, but it is an extremely strong tale, one that calls for interpretation. Because folktales provide meaning on a number of different levels at the same time, no one of these interpretations is conclusive.

THE MORALISTIC OVERLAY

"Be a good girl, don't stray from the path, make sure nothing bad happens to you." This sermon is the first thing that strikes us about the tale. Little Red Cap is warned about the wolf, and thus about men and their sex drives. Perrault[13] made this warning especially clear; in his "moral" of the story, he wrote that young women should be especially wary of the gentle wolves, who are the worst of all; they lure girls tip-toe into their rooms . . . Often considered the original version, Perrault's tale ends when Little Red Cap and her grandmother are devoured. There is no liberation from the belly of the wolf.

The view that sees the wolf as a sexually driven man who takes no responsibility for his greed stands in an ancient tradition of interpretation. While logical enough, it is not the only possible interpretation. The wolf need not necessarily be masculine.

The final scene of the Grimms' version culminates in the hunter getting the wolf's fur, the grandmother getting her wine and cakes, and Little Red Cap taking a vow: Never again will she stray from the path; from now on she will do exactly as her mother says. Little Red Cap might just as well have stayed in the belly of the wolf.

Yet even if we view the tale through the lens of this moral overlay, an important issue does emerge: the girl's ties to her mother, her attempts to free herself, and her failure to do so. We witness what happens when the ties to the mother are not cut. The story recommends not cutting these ties. At what price?

INNOCENT VICTIM, INSIDIOUS CULPRIT

A second interpretation deals with a conflict between an innocent and naive victim (Little Red Cap) and a sly, insidious culprit (the wolf). Many artists and thinkers have understood and recast the story in these terms.[14] The encounter between Little Red Cap and the wolf is broadened to encompass the universal theme of a confrontation between victim and aggressor. Brezhnev referred to this theme[15] when he said that those are deluded who believe that Yugoslavia is Little Red Cap and the Soviet Union is the lecherous wolf.

The many interpreters who have Little Red Cap emancipate herself contribute less to the emancipation of women than to that of the victim. As a victim, Little Red Cap can just as easily portray the plight of man. Both Little Red Cap and the wolf can represent unbalanced attitudes that need to be adjusted, whether on the part of men or women. For instance, a man is just as likely as a woman to fall into the trap of letting someone else manage his life, offering no resistance, pretending that it is for his own good, until suddenly one day he is seized by a violent rage.

Of course, the relationship itself between man and woman can be seen in terms of the "innocent victim—insidious culprit" paradigm, that is, in terms of rape. Little Red Cap can be rewritten to serve this purpose as well.

Unfortunately, such new versions simply exchange one evil for another. Little Red Cap now shoots the wolf dead. Nothing is gained by this maneuver. The story offers no solution. Unlike other folktales, Little Red Cap still provides no clue as to how victim and aggressor might deal with each other in a more productive way. Now the moral of the story really can be reduced to a warning about wolves and innocence. Here we return to the girl who "stays with the mother," avoids transformation, dodges the emotional tasks that belong to her stage of life. It is hard to see any wisdom about relationships in a "Red Cap" who stays "little."[16]

More recent interpretations dealing with the confrontation between aggressor and victim attempt to bring the wolf and Little Red Cap to a table of reconciliation. For example, the wolf is asked why he is so greedy. These attempts arise out of the insight that victims can easily become aggressors, and that we must balance out the victimized parts of ourselves with the aggressive parts of our being.

TOWARD A MORE DEPTH-PSYCHOLOGICAL INTERPRETATION

The story begins by introducing mother, child, and grandmother. We find ourselves in a realm of mothers. No mention is made of fathers or men. They are either missing or have been excluded.

The tale's task is to show how a relationship to the masculine can commence. On the objective level, this would be a capacity to relate to a man. On the subjective level, it would be a relationship to one's own masculine qualities. Folktales convey the hope that the masculine and feminine dimensions of our being can cooperate. They convey the conviction that this rapport is conducive to the successful management of life's passages, and that masculine or feminine qualities can be developed to meet the needs of a specific crisis. In this story, an urgent call for masculine virtues goes out in order to free the restrictive bonds to the mother.

Little Red Cap is introduced as a "sweet young thing" whom everyone is fond of. Thinking of how to fulfill her heart's desire, Grandmother gives her the little red cap made of velvet. Here enough information is provided to account for the secret of Little Red Cap's charm among both mothers and daughters—and to account for the rage of daughters who do not care to stay in the role of the good little girl. Yet who does not wish to be loved so intensely by everyone? And who does not want to have such a well-behaved daughter? Although I am generally in favor of spunk and verve rather than sweetness and goodness, it is not so easy to get completely free of this ideal image of the good little girl.

The red cap has inspired many amplificatory excursions. Red is a color that signals, calls attention to itself, calls attention to those who wear it, to those who want to signal something, and who are thus not in a good position to hide. Red is also a color of spirit, vitality, aggression, energy, and blood. There may be here a reference to the first menstruation. Providing her with a signature of her own, the grandmother's bequeathing of the cap invests Red Cap with importance. In view of the fact that red is often associated with the love goddess, we are being told that it is time for Little Red to get away from Mother and face up to the world of Eros.

These three women could also represent the trinity of the Great Goddess, who appeared in prehistoric Europe in three hierophanies[17]: the girl as goddess of the springtime, the goddess of the summer in the form of the love and earth goddess, and the goddess of winter, death, the underworld, and wisdom. White corresponds to the goddess of spring, red to that of summer, and black to the goddess of winter.

We could thus imagine Little Red Cap making her way from the goddess of spring to the goddess of summer. Grandmother provides the initial push in this direction. Psychologically, the rotation of seasons suggests that she must grow, and all growth involves both death and rebirth. The time has come for a transformation of her feminine identity, and this can happen only by going in one direction: away from her personal mother, toward her grandmother, to the beginnings of the motherline.

There is a strange inconsistency here in the story: mother treats daughter like a little girl, and yet the red cap indicates sexual maturation. This gave authors such as Bettelheim[18] the occasion to speak of premature menstruation. I am more inclined to view the mother as protecting her daughter too long, and thus keeping her from taking her own path of personal development.

From the girl's perspective, the story tells of a mother who treats her daughter like a small child as long as she can, protecting her from life. The time has come for her to become a woman. The mystery of feminine maturation has often been envisioned as the death of a girl who is then reborn as a woman. She must make the transition from a condition of growing, showing promise for the future, and being held to one of holding, being, and exercising maternal care for herself, others, and nature.

A much simpler scheme for this transition (in the language of folktales) would have consisted of entering the woods (and thus mother nature), where she would meet either a beautiful prince or an "animal bridegroom"—an animal by day and a prince at night.[19] It would take a stretch of the imagination to see the vicious wolf that Little Red Cap meets as a prince in disguise.

The wolf, far from noble, embodies a "principle of greed." When he is hungry, he is cunning, can be nasty and aggressive, looks for a fight he can win. The wolf is also a symbol for ravaging death. Little Red Cap is overtaken by a desire in animal form. It is an energy that does not shy from attacking, grabbing, and destroying. This barbaric behavior is celebrated by the wolf in response to Little Red Cap's questions: seeing, hearing, grabbing, and eating are the things he does well. And yet although his aggression is far from civilized, he does voice his desires in human language.

Before displaying his naked desire, the wolf shows that he has a tender side. He charms Little Red Cap with his hymn to the flowers and birds. Here the wolf is a romantic nature mystic who seduces her with his poetic raptures. Luring her off the straight and narrow path, he frees her from her ethic of duty. Is this maneuver designed only to win him time?

If we view the wolf as an aspect of Little Red Cap's personality, we see what happens when her mother stops trying to control her: She meets in the wolf part of her nature, the part of herself that she had denied: a Red Cap who is dreamy, and aggressive, desperate, and dangerously greedy in her search for life, the Little Red Cap who keeps on going for more flowers. As a wolf she gets to know a side of herself that is "loose," that doesn't care about duties or about what others think about her. The story moralizes that this sort of thing is dangerous, although so far she has done nothing worse than enjoying the pleasures of strolling, admiring the flowers, discovering the sensuality of nature both around and within her. But leaving the beaten path to do her own thing also expresses her disdain of convention. Her mother had expressly forbidden her to stray from the tried and true way, but this very act of forbidding made Red Cap realize that there was something unique for her to discover for herself. Mothers are always left in the dust when we go our own way.

Red Cap's mother puts her in a double bind: she is supposed to go by herself, but she is not supposed to go her own way. This quandary confronts every parent. Who wants to prevent one's child from discovering what life is all about? And yet who can simply sit back and let it happen, come what may? Who does not know the tension between wanting things to take their own course, and yet also wishing that they could stay the way they are for a while?

While Red Cap is busy gathering flowers, the wolf is occupied devouring Grandma. Red Cap can also be seen as part of the grandmother's personality. Obsessed by the desire to have the granddaughter in her presence, she is devoured by the principle of greed.

Her possessive love is suffocating. She is hungry, like the wolf. This image warns of the dark side of maternal love, a possessive, smothering desire to have and to hold. It might be comfortable in the belly of the wolf, but it is a rather constricted existence. There is not much light, not much contrast, not much happening. One could only hope that something might happen that would get one out of there.

At the level of relationship, this would describe a child who is overprotected, who has to ask her parents before she can do anything, who is brainwashed by her mother and father. As a description of her inner psychology, the chamber of the wolf's belly represents a state of depression or addiction. The ego complex is too weak to withstand the beck and call of the unconscious.

What is needed to get out of this impasse is a man who is practiced in using his aggression. To fill this need the hunter appears in the tale. His presence has been sorely missed, but once he is there, he does not bring about a change overnight, because no one is ready to make the kind of lasting commitment to the masculine that would be necessary in order to grow out of the exclusive ties to Mother, end the safety of complying with her, and reach a greater degree of personal autonomy. Little Red Cap goes back to her mother and promises to obey from now on—a tragic ending! No transformation takes place.

The image of the grandmother in the belly of the wolf gives us a clue. Living among the oaks and the hazelnut bushes, the grandmother seems to be of Druid origin. Enjoying her traditional wine and cakes, she embodies the Great Mother: the story has the wolf devouring no less than the Great Mother herself. The masculine, having been excluded from the feminine mysteries of fertility and transformation, devours the feminine and grants himself the right to give birth. Snipping Little Red Cap and her grandmother out of the belly of the wolf is a Caesarean birth.

Freud[20] considered whether the wolf might secretly embody a feminine principle. Might this scene express a fantasy of death and rebirth? This could be true without abandoning the perspective of the wolf as a masculine usurper of the Great Mother.[21] The man as wolf would like to be able to do what she does, without her. In this case the folktale, like so many others, would deal with the often violent transition from a matriarchal to a patriarchal order.

In our time, the appropriation of the Great Mother has become a way of life. We profit daily from having assumed responsibility for her processes. It is no accident that the "exploitation of nature" has become a household expression, which, like most household expressions, doesn't change very much. Technology has even provided previously imaginable means by which human fertility and reproduction can be manipulated. It has all but "devoured" feminine wisdom concerning the cycle of death and rebirth, marginalizing intuitive traditions devoted to natural growth. Of course, it is not only men who want to overthrow the Great Mother; since they dwell in the same Zeitgeist, both men and women are equally responsible. They are both victim and culprit. But concern for the Great Mother does seem to be more natural for women. They are generally not as threatened by her power. The pre-Hellenic Great Goddess, for instance, has attracted a great deal of interest among scholars and laywomen. Detailed descriptions of her, some of which may be somewhat idealized, have provided many women with the opportunity to take more seriously the experiences and feelings associated with her. They locate this experience next to that of masculine thought. Men too are increasingly considering their feminine side more seriously as a dimension of holistic living and thinking.

In the folktale, Little Red Cap must see through the wolf, but her innocence prevents her. We often ask ourselves if we are too naive and blind to the things that happen around us. Red Cap does pose the famous questions, "But Grandma, why are your . . . ?" She does give voice to her doubts. But is it enough to doubt?

We have explored thus far two interpretive possibilities. On a personal level, we see a girl who is well protected by her mother and who constellates a constricting mother complex, a girl who needs to grow out of her innocence. Her mother has taken better than good care of her, and she has no relationship with any father. The masculine principle does not come to expression as a friendly helper or a courageous prince, as we might expect from a folktale, but rather as a wolf. In general, the masculine principle (available to both men and women), when it is awakened and becomes integrated, can show the way out of symbiosis.[22] But in this story this does not happen. What happens is a tragic finale in which everything is devoured by greed and fantasy, a kind of medieval morality play portraying the jaws of hell.

The other mode of interpretation is less personal and more cultural. Patriarchal values that were excluded from the feminine mysteries plot to take over the matriarchy. A similar historical process can be seen in the myth of Demeter and Persephone.[23]

Demeter, as we have said of Red Cap's mother, is the earth goddess who is not willing to surrender her daughter. And Kore, like Red Cap, was abducted while picking flowers. Kore's abductor Hades might be compared in his rapacious hunger with the wolf. But once Hades has Kore in the underworld, he falls in love with her and marries her—which has no parallel in the Red Cap tale. Devastated by the loss of her daughter, Demeter puts a stop to all growth, forcing Zeus to intervene in underwordly affairs. From now on, Kore must spend three months in the underworld as Persephone, Hades's wife, and is allowed to spend nine months in the upper world with her mother. This forced marriage is another mythic echo of a patriarchal takeover of the feminine fertility mysteries. The underworld in the Demeter myth could be compared to the belly of the wolf in the Red Cap tale.

The myth, unlike the tale, proposes a solution to this no-win situation: Persephone becomes pregnant in the underworld. There is nothing like this in the folktale; Little Red Cap does not marry the hunter, nor does anything change either in the relationship between women and men, nor between feminine and masculine principles.

Therapists are often faced with clients who have an attitude similar to that of Red Cap. In working with the "Red Cap syndrome," we would want to find out what a woman needs to do to leave her mother without being devoured body and soul by the wolf. A more contemporary mentality has spawned the invention of new solutions in the form of rewritten versions of the folktale. A certain historical shift of consciousness has taken place that allows Red Cap and the wolf to meet on different terms from those prescribed by the somewhat old-fashioned tale. Less naive, Little Red Cap has become more emancipated from her mother complex.

THE RELATION OF THE TALE
TO THE ANALYSAND'S BIOGRAPHY

Angela had to deal in a very immediate way with matters that have been described more theoretically: she had to provide her own meeting ground for Little Red Cap and the wolf. Angela had to expose herself to risk. She found a resonance in the necessity of mother and daughter letting go of each other that was expressed in the tale. And she experienced this process of gaining independence in relation to her therapist as well. To achieve this, she had to get in touch with a highly aggressive masculine energy that she encountered both within and apart from herself. At a yet deeper level of her being, Angela experienced a transformation of her feminine identity.

Angela was considering whether or not to have a child. This metamorphosis of her identity could well amount to a kind of death and rebirth for her, which would arouse a great deal of anxiety. Musing on the tale, Angela once remarked, "The wolf swallowed up my father," a reference to her father's death when she was four years old. In Angela's mind, the memory of her father's death was associated with the fear of being devoured by a strange being. We are reminded that the Great Goddess was also a goddess of death.

Angela is affected by a problem that in our times encroaches on all of us from two sides: we can neither afford to be naive (e.g., by identifying exclusively with the Great Mother in the style of some feminists), nor can we afford to be "bad" and "anti"—devoured by wolves. The only way through this Scylla and Charybdis is via the expansion of personal autonomy, a process of emotional growth that draws on both the Great Mother and the wolf.[24]

The tale speaks to one of Angela's chief problems. Thanks to her good relationship with her mother, her mother complex was basically a positive one. She always feels rich, no matter how poor she is, always sees the flowers along the way, always manages to find a place for herself in the world, including apartments and jobs when she needs them. The world is not a hostile place to her. Like Little Red Cap, she is just a little naive. She sees no evil, and though others may be unkind, at least *she* is nice most of the time. Her inner world of fantasy is also a safe place.

The only thing that ripples her calm is a fear of death. Having experienced the death of her half-sister at an early age, she was sure when she was young that she would die before she had a chance to make love with a man. But this morbid fantasy was covered over by her desire to live.

Angela's aggression was not freely at her disposal, which caused her a certain amount of anxiety. Within her family, her brother was the one who was given responsibility for being aggressive; Angela took on the job of being anxious. This required that she stay on hold. No fascinating men came to Angela to rouse her from her mother-bound slumbers.

There was one man in Angela's life, but he was someone for whom the wolf was just as much of a problem as it was for her. If she had been able to profit from a confrontation with the wolfish part of herself, she might have allowed him the chance to let his wolfish side out to play and discover itself. But this experiment was blocked owing to the risk in her psyche of being overwhelmed by patriarchal tendencies. She had great difficulty remaining herself in the presence of overbearing men. As a woman, she suddenly felt like a nothing. In such moments, it was as if the Great Mother had been swallowed. All feminine power left her. No image remained to remind her of what it would be like to be a strong woman standing up to a strong man.

For Angela, it would not suffice to enter into an external relationship to the masculine. The question was whether she would be able to find a relationship to the masculine within herself. Those men who so towered over her in reality had a foothold in the inner masculine parts that limited her self-esteem. When those inner parts became activated, they made her feel like a little girl.[25]

Angela's choice of a research topic for a paper she wrote during her studies shows how intensely engaged she was with the theme of being threatened by her mother complex and of remaining a girl who is unable to take the next step in her development. She chose a fairy tale in which an old mother devours a young mother.

WAYS TO GROW BY WORKING
WITH THE FOLKTALE

When working with favorite folktales, I try to encourage a playful encounter with its motifs, especially those that have had a particular impact on the memory of the person concerned.

At first Angela simply dwelled on the folktale. As she began to gather associations, she recalled things from her past. Gradually she narrowed her focus to particular motifs. Here she applied the methods of Imagination, Active Imagination, and painting. Imagination is a technique in which images of things that have vanished from memory or that have not yet been defined can be summoned to consciousness, where they are examined and tailored to fit. Such images have a life of their own. The degree of life that they are allowed depends on the degree of free-floating anxiety. With anxiety at a minimum, images and figures emerge, come alive, speak. Active Imagination provides the added element of the ego complex's attempt to take up a conscious relationship to the figures that arise. In the process, these figures undergo change—as does the ego complex. These psychological changes manifest themselves in variations of mood and affect.[26] Angela created the following Imagination:

> Little Red Cap fantasy just before falling asleep: I see a rebellious and defiant Little Red Cap. In fact, she is even violent. She slits open her grandmother's belly. I am afraid of these fantasies, and stop them.
>
> Two days later. Little Red Cap is on her way to her grandmother's house. She is carrying a large basket filled with food and wine. The basket is heavy. Little Red Cap knows the way well. But today she is not at all in the mood to go. "Why do I always have to visit Grandmother? I wish I could just play with the other kids." She comes to a clearing in the forest. "I like this place. The sun is shining so nicely. I think I'll just lie down here and daydream a little. I don't want to go any further down the path. I don't want to go through the dark part of the forest. It is always so scary. I think I'll just stay here in the sun for a while." Little Red Cap lies in the sun and lets herself drift off into dreamland. Suddenly she feels the presence of someone close by. She is startled and opens her eyes. It is the wolf. "What are you doing today?" the wolf asks. "Aren't you going to visit your grandmother?" His voice is pleasant. His eyes sparkle with cunning. Little Red Cap likes this. "Would you like to come with me?" asks the wolf. "You would like it in our den. It's not boring there like it is at home and at your grandmother's house. You'll have plenty of time to play. You'll like the cubs." Little Red Cap thinks it over. "This basket is so heavy, and I have such a long way to go. I'm not at all in the mood to see Grandmother. And I don't feel like going home either. My mother always sends me into this forest. Lately she has always been so depressed, and it's so boring at Grandma's house." The wolf says, "If you come with us, you will lose your fear of the forest. You will feel safe with us." Little Red Cap jumps to her feet. "O.K., I'm coming with you. Help me carry this heavy basket."

At last Angela has been able to ventilate a toxic fantasy about her grandmother. She makes friends with the fascinating wolf. As she becomes defiant, she becomes less destructive.

Has Angela disarmed the wolf by means of her fantasy? Has she integrated him? In order to find out, I invite Angela to speak in the role of Red Cap speaking to the wolf. The second time she does this, the wolf takes the form of a friend who invites her to come and play with him in a pleasant place.

Angela is now invited to take the role of the wolf and of Little Red Cap. She observes:

> As Red Cap I am at ease, not afraid. As the wolf I feel heavy, furry, on my guard. It is hard for me to talk to Red Cap. I feel stiff and heavy—comfortably heavy.

Reflecting on this Imagination, Angela realizes that she is afraid of her wolf. She is afraid of herself as a wolf. Angela becomes upset with herself. "For once, I could get mad," she scolds herself, "but I can't, because I'm too afraid of my own aggression. I can't be assertive like the wolf." She feels lame. Considering what she does to her grandmother in her fantasy, it is no wonder she is afraid of the wolf within her. The feeling of being lame, which Angela sometimes experienced in groups, could now be seen in the light of her swollen aggression and its inhibition.

Later Angela made another Imagination in which she gave the wolf her red cap and received three hairs in return. The wolf hair would help her if she got into trouble.

> One day Little Red Cap comes home from her grandmother's house. Now she has a bicycle, which she enjoys riding very much, and which makes it substantially easier to get around. She meets the wolf in the usual place. The wolf runs along beside her part of the way. "Stop, Red Cap," says the wolf. "I want to ask a favor." Red Cap is not so easy to slow down. She stops at the edge of the forest.
>
> "What do you want from me, wolf?"
>
> "I want your red cap. Won't you please give it to me? I'm going to bury it in a secret place. You can have three hairs from my neck."

Although it is hard to part with her favorite hat, she agrees. The wolf instructs her in how to remove the hairs: she should stroke his neck against the grain. More than three hairs come off on the back of her hand. "You can only keep three of them," he tells her. Red Cap takes a small can out of a basket that her grandmother once gave her and puts three of the hairs in it.

Now Red Cap has the three hairs from the wolf. She keeps them in the little can, her favorite gift from her grandmother. She is not quite sure why she keeps them in the can. They just seem to belong there.

I'm going to the city. I have to get away, can't stay here another minute. Have to leave this place. I'm going to the chimney sweeper's house. How do I know? I just know. I know where his house is, even though I've never been there before. It's on the edge of town. The chimney sweeper has a large black dog. He lives alone. He is a hermit.

I knock on his door. "Come in." I open the door. A man is sitting at a table, head in hands. Can't see his face. I think it is dark outside. Want to leave again. He seems to sense this. "Stay here." Just as I think of the wolf hairs in my bag, I have the feeling that my eyes are flaring up. "Why should I stay if I don't like it here?" "Where else have you got to go?" "I'll find a place to go, all right, but first I want to have a look around here."

In this Imagination Angela meets a number of depressed men, all of whom try to gain control over her. Naturally, they are an expression of her own depression and the way it robs her of her psychic energy. This is most likely to happen when she cannot utilize her aggression to honor and realize her wishes and needs. The wolf hairs gave her the will to fight. The depressed men could not keep her captive. Her eyes flare up. She has taken on a bit of the wolf.

The image of wolf hair occurs in other folktales. The hair has the power and character of the wolf himself. Those who help a wolf or get in touch with the wolfish part of themselves are given the hair as the sign that they have access to their inner wolf potential. Symbolically, it makes good sense that Red Cap trades her hat for the hair. With her will to fight, she is a changed woman. The hair of the wolf gives her what she needs to locate "strange and depressed" men (as she called them) without getting involved. The change that she went through was also visible in a picture that she painted. Titled *Red Zora* (see figure 1), the picture was of a young woman who replaced the little girl. Red Cap is no longer little. Red Zora is a character from a novel for young people by Kurt Held. In the novel Zora takes care of herself and an entire gang, saving their lives. The gang seems tough and ready for a fight. Zora's red hair portrays her wildness and belligerence. To those who don't know her, she seems like a kind of demon. Angela finds Zora important enough to paint her.

In another Imagination, Angela stands up to the hunter.

"Who were you talking to, Red Cap?" says the hunter. "You really ought to keep your eyes on the road. Your mother is waiting for you to come home."

"Why shouldn't I have a good time? You wouldn't believe it if I told you who I was talking to."

"Who? To yourself?"

"No, the wolf!"

"Are you out of your mind, letting that beast in? You have no idea how dangerous that is."

"I'm not sure who is more dangerous: you or the wolf. You hunt the same animals; you even carry a gun. Doesn't that make you feel as strong as the wolf?"

The hunter is angry. "You have no respect. The way you talk to people!"

It is all that Red Cap can do to keep from spitting at the hunter. "I really dislike this guy. He is always full of his own good advice. I've had enough." Red Cap speeds away on her bike.

The hunter, an authority figure who represents the mother's moral outlook, has been dethroned. A shorter Imagination about a young man with blond hair brings this fantasy to a provisional close.

I hear someone whistle, look out the window. Down below is a young fellow whose blond hair shines in the dark. He looks scruffy. Black pants and a yellow sweater. Hair sticking out in tufts.

"Come down the back stairs. I've been watching you. I know you want to get out of here."

"How do you know? What makes you think I want to come with you?"

"I like you. Come with me and my friends. We'll stir up some trouble downtown. I promise it won't be boring."

The wolf has been replaced by a spirited youth. This young animus figure seduces her into participating in very youthful behavior—Angela is thirty-eight.

Emotional equilibrium has not been reached yet. On one side are old, depressed animus figures. On the other side is a very adolescent figure.

But the intrapsychic couple has undergone a significant change. Little Red Cap and the wolf have been replaced by Red Zora and A Youthful Hero. The second couple is much more balanced and likely to survive than the former. They can fight better.

What gains did Angela make from playing with the Little Red Cap story? She wrote:

Little Red Cap lost her innocence. My inner redness began to flow. For days on end I felt a vibrant, warm, red feeling in my body. Am I pregnant with Red?

I feel like I had a very real encounter with the wolf. The wolf should not be killed, as in the traditional story. The wolf has something for me that is very strong and fierce. The wolf can face the elements. I see him "pacing the lonely woods."

The wolf also represents an important capacity for the strange and lonely men that came up in my Red Cap fantasies. The wolf has not yet caught up with them. The Red Zora cap could help them make the connection. I also have the feeling that a piece of my "forgotten past" has come alive again. Before doing this work, I felt as if Red Cap had gone off the path and had gotten lost.

Red Cap is playful. As I was reading through my fantasies

again, I felt I was getting reacquainted with a part of me that is spirited, fleet of foot, ready to play and to get side-tracked.

How did work with this favorite story help with a diagnosis of Angela's structure of complexes? The changes that Red Cap went through in relation to the wolf forestalled the traditional tragic ending. This may not eradicate the archetypal background consisting of a death mother and a rapacious masculine figure. But a Red Cap who has undergone transformation no longer needs to let herself be devoured. She has become a little less apt to fall back into the role of the innocent little girl on her way to visit her grandmother.

Within the framework of her therapy, the work with the story helped Angela to take a step forward in her personal autonomy. As a result, she felt increasingly able to take responsibility for her life. At times when giving in would have been easier, and wrong, she felt prepared to assert herself.

THE BRAVE LITTLE TAILOR

Identifying with the Hero of a Folktale

What happens if an identification with a hero from a favorite child-hood story never dissolves, and continues into adulthood? Here is an example of what happened to one particular person.

A forty-five-year-old man seeks therapy in the wake of his third divorce. At first impression, he seems rather sad and inflexible, which is accented by his large frame and posture. His vocabulary contains a sizeable proportion of such words as "order," "orderly," "guidelines," "progress." He complains of having a hard time finding warmth in relationships, a sacrifice in his personal life that he blames on his professional success. Could it be that others were afraid of him? He admits that he demands excellence from his employees, but sees himself as an understanding boss. Yes, there must be discipline. No, nothing escapes his watchful eye. In my consulting room he spoke as if he were addressing an audience filling an entire lecture hall. I asked him if he was aware that he was speaking with such volume. Was he afraid I might not hear him otherwise? Dazed, he told me that was how he always talked, and then continued on. I felt as if there weren't enough room for both of us, and caught myself looking for some way of changing the atmosphere. Unfortunately, nothing occurred to me.

When I asked him what had happened to bring about his suc-cessive divorces, he replied that his wives had found him to be intolerably authoritarian. He wanted to be admired, and kept them well informed of how much he was earning in order to assure himself of this attention, but apparently this lost its appeal after a while. His wives had also found him to be rigid and unimaginative. In the beginning they had appreciated his inflexibility for the stability it seemed to offer, but after a while it was too much to take. All of his previous wives agreed that he had treated them as property without the least bit of sensitivity. He reported all this to me without noticeable emotion.

When I asked him about memories from childhood, he told me he recalled a folktale his father always used to tell him, "The Brave Little Tailor." This story was very important for him, and his father had told it to him again and again. His father was a worker who wanted his son "to have it better." When he was five years old, a friend told his father that his son would achieve something great. He was convinced his son was extraordinarily gifted, and his son agreed. This pact resulted in a highly motivated individual. But "The Brave Little Tailor" was a story that his father had told him much earlier than he had talked about professional success. My analysand could still recall the story vividly. And as a matter of fact, he told it to me right then and there in the analytical hour. He told it with immense detail, including the part where a pig is captured in the chapel. He concluded, "And then the tailor married the princess. The end."

All of this took place in the first session. The stiltedness of the conversation quickly ended as soon as he began telling the story of "The Brave Little Tailor."

THE STORY[27]

One summer morning, a tailor was sewing at his table by the window. Outside in the street a farmwoman came toward him calling out, "Fine jam for sale! Fine jam for sale!" The tailor liked the sound of that. He stuck his little head out of the window and called to her, "Come up here, dear woman, I'll help you get rid of some of that." When she got to the top of the stairs, the little fellow persuaded her to take out every single jar in her basket so he could have a look. In the end he bought only a quarter pound. The woman went away grumbling.

"Let God bless this jam," said the little tailor, "and give me health and strength." He sliced a piece of bread lengthwise and spread the jam on it. "You are going to be very tasty," he said, "but before I bite into you, I just want to finish sewing this vest." He put the bread down beside him and began sewing oversized stitches in eager anticipation of his dessert. Meanwhile, the fragrance of the jam wafted up the walls to the flies, who came down in droves to light on it. When the tailor saw all the unwanted guests, he said, "Hey, who invited you?" and swept them away. But the flies didn't understand English, and rather than allow themselves to be shooed away for long, they quickly returned, with their friends. The tailor then blew his top. He took the rag hanging under his sink and whacked them with it. "Take that!" When he pulled away the rag he found seven flies lying dead with their legs sticking up in the air. "Not bad," he said, admiring his deed. "This should make the headlines." In no time flat, he sewed himself a pouch to tie around his waist and stitched large embroidered letters on it that said, "Seven in one blow." "Headlines are not enough; the whole world should hear about this!" His heart wagged with joy like the tail of an eager dog.

Putting on his pouch, he scoured his house for something to eat that he could take with him on his big adventure. All he could find was an old hunk of cheese, so he tucked it in his pouch. By the gate he was lucky enough to catch a bird, which he also tucked in his pouch. Soon he had gathered his courage and was on his way up a steep mountain. At the top he saw a huge giant. "Hello, friend," he said to the giant. "You look like you'd like to see some of the world. That sounds good to me. How would you like to join me?" The giant just looked at him and said, "You poor fool." "Oh yeah? Take a look at this," said the tailor as he untied his pouch and showed it to the giant. "If you could read this you might change your mind." When he read "Seven in one blow," the giant immediately assumed that it referred to people, and began to show a little more respect. But he wasn't yet completely convinced, and so he thought of a test to find out if it was true. He took a stone in his fist and squeezed it *so hard that drops of water came out of it.* "Do that, if you think you are so strong." "No problem," said the tailor. "Watch."

He fished the hunk of rotten cheese out of his pouch and squeezed it until the juice ran out of it. "See?" he said. "I got more out of mine." Taken aback by what the tailor could do, the giant didn't know what to say. So he took a stone and threw it so high up into the sky it vanished out of sight. "O.K., squirt, do that." "Right away, sir," the tailor replied. "That was a good throw, but your stone did come back down again. I'm going to throw a stone so high you won't ever see it again." He reached into his pouch, took out the bird, and cast it away. Glad to be set free, the bird soared far into distant skies. "What do you think, my friend? How did you like that?" "Well, you may be able to throw," said the giant. "But let us see what you are worth when it comes to carrying." He picked up a massive oak tree that was lying on the ground. "Let's carry this together out of the forest." The little man quickly added, "Good. You take the trunk on your shoulders, and I'll take the top with all the branches, which is much bigger and heavier." The giant lifted the trunk onto his shoulder. The tailor scrambled right up into the branches and sat down. So the giant ended up carrying everything, including the tailor.

The tailor enjoyed himself and whistled all his favorite tunes, as if this were mere child's play. It wasn't long before the giant was completely exhausted. "Stop," he pleaded. "I have to put it down." The tailor jumped down and put his arms around the tree as if he had been carrying it the whole time. "You mean a big guy like you can't even carry that little sapling?" Next they came to a cherry tree. The giant reached up, grabbed a branch from the top of the tree where the cherries were ripe, and bent it down for the tailor. Too weak to hold onto it, the tailor was whipped up into the air. "What seems to be the problem? Can't you even hold onto that little sapling?" "What I just showed you," replied the tailor, "is something that can only be done by someone who licked seven in one stroke. Don't you see what happened? Those seven hunters down there are shooting at these bushes. That's why I flipped myself over the tree. See if you can do that!" Trying to snap himself over the tree, the giant got all tangled up in its branches, once again proving the tailor's superiority. "Come and spend the night with us giants in our cave," said the giant.

The tailor accepted the invitation, and when they arrived at the cave, the giant showed him a bed to sleep in. But rather than lying down in it, the tailor made himself comfortable in a niche. At midnight the giant came in with a slab of iron and hammered the bed where he assumed the tailor would be sleeping. One good blow, he thought, and that will be the end of the little twerp. The next day the giants went into the forest and would have forgotten all about the tailor if he hadn't walked up to them all cocky and full of himself. Shocked and afraid that he would knock them all dead, the giants scattered in all directions.

The tailor continued on his way, following his pointy nose, until he came into the courtyard of a castle. Exhausted, he lay down in the grass and fell asleep. As he was lying there, the king's courtiers came and looked him over, and noticed his pouch on which it was written, "Seven in one blow." "My," they exclaimed, "what is this great warrior doing here in times of peace? He must be a mighty warlord." They went straight to the king to report what they had found. If war should break out, the tailor could be of great use to them. They could not afford to let him go. The king took their advice, and sent someone to offer the tailor employment as soon as he awoke. "Of course I will," answered the tailor. "That is precisely why I am here. I would like to offer my services to the king." So they received him in style and assigned him a special residence.

This treatment displeased the other soldiers, and soon they were cursing him. "If he takes seven in one blow, how is it going to make us look? We'll look like weaklings next to him." So they decided to go to the king and inform him of their departure from the legion. "We're not going to fight together with a superman." The king regretted losing all of his good men just for the sake of this one. He wished he had never set eyes on him, and thought about how he could get rid of him. But he didn't dare dismiss him for fear he might retaliate, striking him and all his people down in order to set himself on the throne.

After taking a long time to make up his mind, he sent a messenger to make a request. Since it had become clear what a mighty war hero he was, he should be pleased to do the royal highness this favor. In a forest within the confines of his kingdom there were two giants who were wreaking great havoc, plundering and murdering with fire and sword. No one had been able to get near them. He could arm himself however he pleased, and if he could kill them, the king would give him his daughter's hand, along with half of the kingdom as a wedding gift. To help him, he would have the services of a hundred knights.

"Just my cup of tea," thought the tailor. "The beautiful princess and half the kingdom. I can't wait." "I agree," he announced. "I'll take care of the giants all right, and your knights can watch. He who can take seven in one blow won't have any trouble with two." Riding out into the forest, he announced to the knights waiting there, "Stay out here, I want to take care of those giants myself."

He went into the forest and looked all around until finally he saw them sleeping and snoring under a tree so that its branches bent with every breath. "This trick is already licked," he thought, filling up his pouch with stones, crawling over the giant and climbing up into the tree. From there he threw stones at his chest, one after the other. Waking up in a fit of rage, the giant yelled at his partner, "Hey, what are you hitting me for?" "You're dreaming," said the other. "I'm not hitting you." Just as they were falling asleep again, the tailor threw another rock at the other one's chest. He jumped up and yelled, "What do you think you are doing? What are you throwing at me?" "I'm not throwing anything," objected the other. After quarreling for a while, they gave up again, since they were so tired, and their eyes fell shut.

The tailor started his game again, taking the biggest rock he could find, throwing it as hard as he could at the first giant's chest. "Now I've had it!" the giant shouted as he leaped to his feet like a madman and punched his friend, who was not about to take that without hitting back. They worked themselves into such a frenzy that they ripped trees out of the ground and pounded each other until both of them were dead.

"I'm sure glad they didn't rip this tree out that I'm sitting in," said the tailor; "otherwise I would have had to make a hasty exit." With a twist of his hips he was down from the tree, drew his sword, made a few elegant stabs into the giants' chests, and returned to his riders. "The giants are lying over there. I bumped them off. That's how it is with someone who strikes seven in one blow. They tore out the trees while they were trying to defend themselves." "You mean they didn't even scratch you?" the riders wanted to know. "Everything went so well," he replied, "they didn't harm a hair on my head." The riders could hardly believe it until they rode into the forest, where they found the giants lying in pools of blood among piles of uprooted trees. Now they were even more amazed and unnerved by the tailor. They had no doubt that he would kill them all if he became their enemy. They rode straight back to the castle and told the king what they had seen. The tailor had arrived too, and announced, "I have come to collect the princess and the half of the kingdom that was promised to me."

The king regretted having made this agreement, and thought of another plan to get rid of the war hero. After all, he had no intention of giving away his daughter. He told the tailor that if he still wanted the princess, he would have to catch a fierce unicorn that had been assaulting people and other animals. Happy to oblige, the tailor took a rope to the edge of the forest, instructing those who were supposed to help him to wait there. He would capture the unicorn himself. He searched everywhere in the forest for the unicorn. Suddenly the beast charged him with his head lowered and his horn aimed at his chest. "Just take it easy," he said to himself, standing still until the animal came closer. As it was about to strike him, he stepped nimbly behind a tree. Unable to stop quickly enough, the unicorn rammed its horn so hard into the tree it couldn't pull it out again, try as it might. It was captured. The tailor came out from behind the tree, tied the rope around the unicorn's neck, and led the unicorn out to his helpers, and then afterward to the king, whom he asked once more to keep his promise.

The king was surprised, but immediately thought of another trick. Before the wedding could be celebrated, the tailor must capture a certain wild pig that was running loose in the forest. The hunters would assist him. "Gladly," said the tailor. "Nothing to it." Once again he went to the edge of the forest, where he left the hunters waiting. They were not displeased, since they had encountered the beast often enough to have no particular desire to see him again. When the pig saw the little man, he charged with foaming mouth and gnashing teeth with every intention of stamping him into the ground. The tailor, who was standing next to a small chapel, at the last possible minute stepped quickly inside. As soon as the pig had followed him into the chapel, he slammed the door closed, and climbed up to a high window and crawled out. The pig was captured, for he could not jump up to the window. After showing it to his hunters, he went to the king. "I caught the pig and the princess at the same time."

It is not difficult to guess what sort of a mood this put the king in. He didn't know what to do. He had to keep his promise and give the tailor his daughter's hand. He really believed that this was a mighty war hero, and had he known that he was actually a tailor, he certainly would have preferred to give him a jacket to sew than his daughter to marry. The marriage ceremony was grand in style but poor in spirit. The tailor was made a king.

It wasn't many nights before the young queen heard the tailor talking in his sleep. "Boy," he said, "make me that vest and patch my pants if you don't want a whacking with this ruler." After hearing this, she knew which side of town her young spouse was from, and she begged the king to help her get free of him. The king soothed her and instructed, "Tomorrow do not lock the door to your room. I'll have some servants take him when he falls asleep." She was comforted by this plan. But the new king's weapon carrier heard everything, and since he was true to his master, he went and informed him. The tailor was not upset. "I'll take care of it." That night he lay down to sleep with his wife at the usual time and pretended to fall asleep quickly. She got up, opened the door, and lay down again. He lay in bed as if still sleeping, and spoke in a high voice, "Boy, make me that vest and patch my pants if you don't want to get a whacking with the ruler. I struck seven in one blow, *killed two giants, caught a unicorn and a wild pig. I wanted those men standing just outside the door to know." When they heard that, they were off and running as if a hundred devils were on their tails. No one ever bothered the tailor again, and he kept his crown until the day he died.*

It is not easy to make up one's mind whether to like or dislike this spunky little tailor. His tricks and wit are entertaining. It is satisfying to see such an insignificant little fellow overcoming such strong and powerful opponents. It is a pleasure to witness intelligence winning out over brute strength.

This story makes a hit among boys and girls of a certain age. Surrounded by "giants," children often identify with the brave little tailor. The story reinforces the child's sense of being able to stand up to these overgrown bullies. And as a matter of fact, children do have a knack for getting what they want from them almost instinctively. Identification with the brave little tailor is a natural.

But there is more to the little tailor than the truism that tricks and cleverness are stronger than strength and force. What about the little tailor's confidence? His calm in the face of adversity is a joy to witness. Nothing can slow him down. No doubt holds him back. In part, this self-assurance expresses the revenge of the proletariat, as Fetscher suggested in his book of satirical folktales, *Who Kissed Sleeping Beauty Out of Her Sleep?*[28] Revolt can also be seen as an intrapsychic process in which elements that had been suppressed are consciously recognized and given a chance to influence actions, after which they work their way into a more dominant position.

Looking more closely at the story, one's enthusiasm for the tailor is dampened by cunning turning into violence. In the end, he has everyone quaking in their boots.

Various sayings have been applied to the story: intelligence is stronger than might; culture is stronger than nature—nature being represented by the giants. Is this message of self-confidence worthy of emulation? The tailor is a "show-off." Those people for whom

"The Brave Little Tailor" was for a time their favorite story add, "But he is a bit too big for his britches." Fascination for this invincible self-confidence is tempered by the anxiety it arouses. It may be necessary to ask ourselves what we thought of the story when we were children, and what we think of it now, after having read it as adults.

The discrepancy between one's feelings as a child and as an adult may be a key to understanding the ambivalence that was at the heart of my analysand's problem. The story accurately mirrored his primary issue. Already in the first few minutes after we met, the theme of power and cunning had come into focus; he spoke as if in a large lecture hall refusing to listen to my questions. I quickly sought a way of tricking him out of his behavior, but was unable to find one.

THE DEPARTURE AND THE GRANDIOSE IDEA

The tailor introduces his modus operandi in the story's first scene. He orders the jam and makes promises that he doesn't keep. Meet the boaster. He sees his own behavior as demonstrating the power of decision—knowing exactly how much he wants, refusing to take a hair more. Rather than letting the farmwoman (a mother figure) manipulate him, he takes advantage of her. One has less sympathy for the tailor's clarity of mind when one puts oneself in the shoes of this woman who has carried her heavy basket all the way up the stairs to sell him only a quarter of a pound. His priorities and lack of empathy for the woman are not very praiseworthy. The tailor's wife at the end of the tale also leaves us with a feeling of pity for someone who has been taken advantage of.

The figure of the tailor appears in many stories. Often portrayed as laborers lacking in physical strength, they possess an inferiority that calls for compensation; often what they are missing in strength they make up for with elegance. "Clothes make the man," and the tailor makes the clothes. In order to "make the man," the tailor has to be able recognize a person's shortcomings. To craft them with his art, he first has to see them as they are. Tailors are responsible for how we present ourselves to others. We call on them to help us create our "persona." They must be schooled in the art of illusion, able to twist and tuck things a little if they are going to be able to help make people better looking than they really are. In folktales, the tailor is as fallible as everyone else, but he should be especially adroit at compensating for his weaknesses. This makes him socially indispensable.

The inner tailor would be a weak, sly, and tricky part of the self that is desperately dependent on recognition from others. The brave little tailor makes of his lucky strike of seven a badge of invincibility. One single stroke of luck immensely boosts his self-confidence. Whether the seven dead bodies are those of flies or warriors is a minor detail; the main thing is that he feels like a hero.

The brave little tailor in us comes alive when we make a real breakthrough and achieve success above and beyond all expectations. A boost in self-esteem endows us with hope and courage to carry us more calmly through the trials that we meet in life. But the tailor shows us how we can be seduced by big ideas. We bite off more than we can chew, and expect more of ourselves than is reasonable. In adulthood, "grandiose" ideas are problematic and pathological, although in childhood they are natural. "I can do anything," a child at the age of five or six may say, and really believe. This conviction gives the child the courage to go out and do something in the world.

A grandiose idea means that we not only know what we want, but that we also have the strength and hope to be able to realize it. In the beginning came the grandiose idea, then came the deed.

In the case of my analysand, it was the father's friend who first fanned the flames of the grandiose idea that the boy was unusually gifted. A fantasy may powerfully awaken self-confidence in a single stroke. If this vision is in touch with reality, good fortune is assured, especially if it is cultivated within the family sphere. If the vision is false, a mere expression of parental wishes that are out of touch with the child's real self and gifts, painful disappointment is guaranteed.

The tailor has a generous portion of self-confidence. He would like to be admired and respected, perhaps even feared. The tailor's way of dealing with the lady selling jam shows what we are up against: the tailor is less interested in food than in power. He seeks admiration and respect to compensate for his sense of inferiority. This opening scene presents us with a symptom of narcissistic pathology that is parallel to a phase of child development, and portrays a "psychology of cunning."

When the tailor's self-confidence is in bloom, he is ready to take on the world. He wants to show that he is somebody. Desire to show others what one can do is more than mere show; it is the root of greater autonomy. The tailor takes this step in stride—if with rather large stitches. Soon he has sewn himself a waist pouch to advertise his heroic deeds. The belt forms a circle that symbolizes energy and a promise of greater integrity. It gives those who wear it power, and may indicate their adherence to a group of ideas. Here it represents commitment to the idea of being a war hero. With it he announces his prowess. But we are well enough informed to know that this heroism is based on a distortion of reality, and that its power of conviction depends on outwitting others. The tailor is mythologically related to such figures as Thor, Siegfried, and Laurin, to all of whom belong power belts that give them the strength of twenty.

The tailor takes whatever he can find—cheese, a bird. He climbs the mountain. Onward and upward. He will have to exert himself to get to the top, but once he has achieved an elevated position he will be able to enjoy looking down on others. There he meets a giant whom he engages in conversation. He tells him about his great plan. The tailor is riding so high he even offers to take the giant with him. But the giant answers back, "You poor fool." We are reminded that this fellow who wants to show the world he is somebody is still a mere tailor. For fear of the world seeing that he is nothing but a "poor fool," he goes to great lengths to show that he is anything but. He is caught in a vicious circle informed by a grandiose idea on one side and an inferiority complex on the other. Convinced that he is nothing but a poor fool, he is possessed by the need to prove himself.

The tailor and the giant engage in a contest, the kind of outer battle that is seductive for persons with unintegrated grandiose selves. The tailor shows how special he can be. He is cocky, creative, and inventive. Luck is on his side. He refuses to use the same weapons as his opponent, for he is quite aware that he is no giant. "I may not be a giant," he seems to be saying, "but whatever you can do, I can do too, maybe even a little better." He demands recognition for his superior performances.

The tailor in us seeks fame and glory by engaging in contests through which we can demonstrate our wits rather than our muscle. The contest expresses an inner struggle with a grandiose idea, the terms of which are set by the "giant." We can translate this to mean that the grandiose idea continually sets the parameters by which we live. This is what we have to wrestle with. The tailor accepts the challenge portrayed by this grandiosity. He shows one possible way to wrestle with it.

What more can this folkloric symbol tell us about grandiosity? Portrayed as strong and stupid, the giant knows nothing but brute force. In other versions, as well as in the second part of the story, he is very emotional. In mythology there are giants of fire and giants of ice, which suggest "gargantuan emotions" that are oversized, blundering, and elemental, making us feel like huge "morons."

The giant expresses the moronic quality of grandiose ideas. Giants in folktales are one-dimensional. The moment he has a feeling, he goes into action and his machinery is not to be stopped. His behavior is predictable. The one-dimensionality of grandiose ideas does not, however, render them less important than more refined ideas. Since grand ideas write the scripts of our lives, we have to grapple with them, for better or worse.

The tailor represents qualities that are a fitting counterpart to the moronic simplicity of the giant. He is creative and able to shift perspectives. He can twist things to his own purposes and has a variety of tricks at his command that are easy to use with someone for whom the giant's behavior is so predictable. The tailor's tricks represent tricks that we all resort to at one time or another. Let us take for example the scene in which he rides on the top of the oak tree, a technique taken from the annals of slave drivers. The tailor gets the giant to do his work for him, prevents him from discovering that he has been manipulated by putting him on the defensive, and then reaps the rewards of his work. Such tricks need to be seen from two different angles. They are clever, but they are also mean.

At the level of mythology, the tailor and giant recall the myth of the "divine child" and the "divine trickster." In myth, when affairs on the face of the earth take a bad turn, a divine child is often sent to set things straight, as for example in the legend of Krishna,[29] who comes when Mother Earth can no longer tolerate the way things are going. Krishna symbolizes the promise of eternal rebirth. These mythological figures are often normal children at the same time as they are notorious tricksters, who perform such deeds as exchanging or doubling herds of cattle. The divine child is always threatened by some demon. It is not difficult to see in this figure an expression of the vulnerability and helplessness of childhood. But the figure also gives expression to the feelings of children who demand greater participation in life, oppose their parents, and criticize them for being too authoritarian or not authoritarian enough.

There is yet more to the mythic image of the divine child. A symbol of new beginnings, the divine child also stands for the creative principle itself, for the possibility and necessity of transformation. It is a psychological law that whenever a creative leap is taking place, a transformation is in process that is not yet impervious to intrusive factors. The old poses a challenge to whatever is new. This is necessary in order for the new thing to stand up and "prove its salt," as the story illustrates.

The tailor is continually being pressured into doing things—by the giants, by the king. His compulsiveness makes me wonder what is wrong with him. His slyness appeals to me, I find his tricks amusing, and I admire his creativity. But I am not convinced that his way of doing things will contribute in the end to a satisfying life—a life, for instance, in which women might also play a part.

His sly wit is remarkable. He is able to start a fight between the giants that leads to their destruction, all the while sitting in a tree out of the fray. A stunt like this reminds us of everyday family occurrences: Junior eats up all the goodies and then quickly finds something for the parents to fight about, or protests, "Dad said that you said . . . " They begin fighting, and Junior deftly removes himself from the scene of the battle.

THE TRIAL

The tailor has a reputation at the king's court. He has his adversaries, who envy, fear, and hate him. The pattern of anxiety and rivalry is repeated, now with the king rather than the giants. No longer ruled exclusively by his grandiose ideas, he has achieved a certain eminence.

If we interpret the king as an independent person rather than a part of the tailor's personality, we see the tailor responding to demands placed on him from his social world. Something is demanded of him besides sly wit. The tailor drew attention to himself with his big ideas; now he has to prove that he can live up to them. The king's plan is clear enough: to do in the tailor, for in this system where power is the name of the game there is no room for a successor. To establish himself here he will have to call on something that he has avoided until now: he will have to show his muscle.

After eliminating the giants with elegant brutality, the tailor, like a toreador, gets the unicorn to run into a tree. He knows that unicorns don't change direction once they fix themselves on a target.

Here is another example of psychological cunning: to be sly we have to be able to understand others, know their weak points, predict their behavior, and act accordingly. Employing this capacity, the tailor disposes of the unicorn without getting his feathers ruffled.

The pig is another occasion for bravado. The tailor runs ahead, the pig chases him, a door closes behind them, and the pig is captured in a chapel. A beautiful dance! The tailor exposes his skin, even risks his life. If he were in therapy, I would tell him the tale "The Man Who Set Out to Learn Fear" (see Kast, 1994). He might be able to learn something from this story. Such a lack of respect for death strikes one as a little strange. Even folktale heroes cannot afford to feel completely immortal. His remarkable tricks do not succeed in completely calming us where trouble is brewing.

The tailor, like the lad in the above tale, has one chief way of dealing with things: to play tricks, outwit—and in the scene with the pig, to catch. One sentence marks the culmination of his thievish wit: "I caught the pig and the princess in one move." Although this sentence allows for more than one interpretation, it is difficult to avoid the impression that he trapped the princess in much the same manner that he trapped the pig. The king is not at all pleased with this move, and the narrative gives no indication of how the tailor and the princess feel about each other. Any mention of love is conspicuously absent.

We have to ask whether anything is gained in the long run by trapping the animal and killing the giants. On the face of it, it is the giants who steal and murder by fire and sword. But perhaps their enormous greed and destructive rage should be attributed to the tailor. If I could suggest a more therapeutic way for the tailor to deal with his shadow, I would have the king send him on a mission to tame, rather than simply to destroy, his greed.

This therapeutic intervention is necessary in relation to the unicorn as well. A mythical creature, the unicorn has often been depicted as a white animal, an ass, rhinoceros, bull, or horse with one horn. According to one ancient legend, the unicorn was the son of a gazelle that mated with a courtesan on the sacred wedding night[30] in order to make rain and fertility, which resulted in the birth of a divine child. According to a later legend, the unicorn could only be tamed in the lap of a virgin, and it was this taming that resulted in the conception and birth of the divine child. The single horn was associated with unrestrained power. The legends make clear that this power can be of a spiritual as well as a sexual nature. We are dealing here with a penetrating force that works on several levels.

Concentrated and focused, it is a force of a very different quality than is represented by the colossal emotionality of the giant, which brings me back to my question: What is accomplished by having the unicorn run into the tree? It seems like a waste of energy. But what happens if we look at the tree trunk as a symbol of the "Great Mother"? It reinforces my suspicion that the tailor's aggression and assertiveness is still locked up in the mother complex, rather than having been freed to the point where he can do something really productive, for the sake of change. Trapped and under control, his wild yet focused instinctual drive has nowhere to go.

The pig is in the same trap. The pig can symbolize fertility as well as happiness. In German, "Schwein haben" ("to have pig") means "to luck out." Mythologically, the swine is a sacrificial animal, sacred to the Mother Goddess Demeter. The pig suffers a certain historical degradation. When mother goddesses were dethroned during the rise of patriarchal cultures, all of the animals associated with them were portrayed as accomplices of devils and witches. Hand in hand with this development was a devaluation and demonization of the body and of sensuality. Our folktale can be seen as an expression of this patriarchal campaign against all traces of the matriarchy. No one would dispute that human beings have a piggish side to their nature, but piggishness need not necessarily be seen as demonic. We can imagine the king sending the tailor on a mission to tame a sex drive that seems to have grown dangerous and out of control. But does this imprisonment of the pig in a chapel really represent a lasting solution? Although a pig enshrined in a chapel suggests the possibility of sublimation, the mode of capture and imprisonment in this story leads me to doubt that a successful sublimation has taken place.

No, I come to a quite different conclusion: the tailor has succeeded in corralling everything of an instinctual nature. He has brought it all under his control. I also find myself forced to the conclusion that this heroic deed affords him nothing in the way of happiness or individuation. His only gain is power. Yes, he wins the hand of the princess, but it is hard to imagine her being terribly enthusiastic about having been "bought." She wonders if he really is who he says he is. And his dreams give away his true identity. At night he returns to the little tailor he was and remains, in spite of all his outward achievements. It is not difficult to predict that the princess will not be overly pleased with him. Justifying her dissatisfaction as disappointment over his lowly social status, she reveals an intense attachment to her father. Power and prestige are at the top of her list too. No way is found for the tailor to make a contribution to the royal lineage. His expertise adds nothing new to the royal court. His ability to terrorize and prove his superiority is remarkable, but it is not much help when it comes to forging relationships.

We could see the princess as an anima figure—an unconscious feminine component of the tailor. The anima is caught in a father complex, whose compulsive fever takes the form of a drive for power, possession, and control. Cunning is enlisted in the service of tyranny. For the anima figure to have any importance in the story, craft would have to have given way to care, tricks to empathy. By the time the tailor reaches the court of the king, we have the right to expect a new and different kind of behavior from the tailor.

THE STORY'S EFFECT IN THERAPY

My analysand reported that up until now he had always been captivated by the little tailor; now suddenly he felt sorry for the giants. I asked him whether this had anything to do with the fact that he himself had become a sort of giant in business. This interpretation met with a resonant response. He did feel like a giant who had to defend himself against all the clever little tailors of the world—there was no way around it. He told me about all the attacks he had fended off, how he had let others do themselves in, usually with refined methods, but sometimes by simply letting them butt their heads directly against his thick hide.

At the outer level, it was clear that he had long identified with the tailor, and in the process had become the giant. He told of the many necessities dictated by circumstance. He had achieved a degree of success, which was not going to maintain itself without his attention. Everything would be fine if it weren't for the women . . .

At an inner level, the battle between the tailor and the giant portrayed his compulsion. He was highly concerned that one of his drives might break loose and get the better of him. This is what drove him to compulsive behavior. His sleeping disorders also fit into this pattern—he had extreme difficulty feeling good enough about himself to relax and stop worrying. In view of the story that was so important in his life, it comes as no surprise that he had little access to the kind of inner resources that would allow him to take a deep breath and trust in things. "You know, actually I am a cheat," he remarked in an unguarded moment.

On his own, he could not recall the ending of the story. So I asked him what he thought about the tailor's relationship with the princess. The tailor had earned her, he thought. I invited him to put himself in her place. His comment: " 'They don't even ask me what I want. What kind of father is that? He's not the least bit interested in me.' She should leave in the middle of the night." He surprised himself. "My lovers always ran away in the middle of the night." "Where did they go?" I asked him. "To the fairies, maybe to Mother Holle. She has bread. Yes, to Mother Holle!"[31] I asked him to describe Mother Holle. "She has a green field, apples, bread, a delicious paradise . . . it is peaceful there."

A decisive change had taken place. By putting himself in the shoes of the princess, he had stumbled on a very clear insight. Suddenly he understood why all the women he had known had left him. He was adamant about telling me what this was like. He wanted to offer them (and thus his feminine side) a special kind of therapy. They should all visit Mother Holle (a personification of the Great Mother). There they would find restoration.

When I tried to get him to return to issues of pressing concern, he resisted, remaining at the level of myth. He seemed to feel more comfortable there. The folktale offered him refuge, which is important and necessary in therapy. The folktale image may provide access to psychic qualities that are unavailable by other means, provided the therapist knows how to work with them.

The analysand repeatedly came back to the idea of a visit with Mother Holle. For instance, he ran the image through his mind while falling asleep. It gradually gave him permission to feel more at peace with himself. In his imagination, he sent all the young women he had been involved with to Mother Holle. Naturally, he accompanied them personally on their travels. Each time he went, he gained greater familiarity with the realm of the Great Mother, and learned what inner tranquility was all about. Each visit allowed him another experience of being immersed in something beside warfare. He learned to lie down and wait until the apples were ripe.

But there was still a question that had not been answered. Why had the story of the brave little tailor maintained its appeal for him long into his adult years? We came to the conclusion that the tailor's tricks were necessary as long as he was still in the process of establishing himself in the world. And we agreed that by the time he entered the king's court, he should have learned a new way of dealing with things. He applied this in his own life to mean that he should have been able to develop a new personal attitude toward himself that would accompany each step forward in his professional life.

Part of his fascination with the brave little tailor was attributable to the universal appeal of the archetypal trickster and divine child. Part of the task of therapy consisted of helping him find a place for this archetype in his life so that it could function creatively for him. We discovered that as a child he had enjoyed participating in dramatic productions, but that he had not pursued his dramatic talents any further because of the minimal financial return that could be expected from it. But the stage had lost none of its appeal, and now in his spare time he began acting again, to his great satisfaction.

When someone has been acting the part of the hero from a favorite fairy tale for so long, therapy usually needs to offer a way for this hero to "grow up." The encounter with Mother Holle allowed my analysand this chance. Therapy should also be able to determine the basic issue embodied by the narrative's protagonist, so that the need it is expressing can be dealt with on a concrete as well as an imaginative level.

In spite of the fact that I am in general critical of the trickster's cunning, I would never deny the necessity of cunning in life. There is no substitute for cunning, because to some extent everyone is weak in the face of immensity. No one is exempt from the need for self-assertion. Survival demands it. But cunning can be applied in different ways at different times. At times it is better to resist the temptation to be clever and devious. There is a direct line from calculation to power to isolation. A strategy for survival that has its own beauty and justification can under certain circumstances be utterly false.

I have chosen to write about this analytic encounter because of the remarkably extended period of deep communication that took place in the intermediating language of the folktale. So many essential issues came to expression in terms of the few tales that were recalled from childhood. It was only toward the end of his therapy, after some seventy hours within a year and a half, that he began to speak more directly about his problems and his relationship with me.

He was convinced that therapy could only take place in "his" language—that is, in the language of the folktale. The safety that he felt in the transitional space of fantasy may have been due to the nature of his relationship with his father. The moments where he recalled hearing his father tell him the story of "The Brave Little Tailor" were moments of the greatest tranquility, acceptance, and hope.

THE SNOW QUEEN

Motifs from Favorite and Dreaded Folktales of Childhood

More often than remembering an entire tale from childhood, we remember only single motifs, motifs that we recall with special fondness—or with particular dread. Some of them were so strange that we never forgot them, and they come back to haunt and inspire us throughout our lives. In therapy, clients may find it easier to tell about particular motifs they remember than to recount entire folktales. Such motifs depict issues that were important in childhood and are still relevant. The moment in which they are recalled indicates the activation of a complex that expresses an issue of current concern (see Kast, *The Dynamics of Symbols*).

If we name all of the motifs that we can think of, we will probably touch on those that are relevant to the passages of our present lives. Others remain in the dark, which may also become activated if the situation requires.

A WAY TO COLLECT MOTIFS

1. List all of the motifs that come to mind.
2. Describe the motifs as closely as possible, relying on memory alone.

3. Compare the motif as remembered with the motif as it occurs in the actual folktale.

4. Take note of which elements have been forgotten and which have been added.

5. Find out which memories are associated with each motif, speculating on their possible meaning.

6. Hypothesize an overall pattern into which the single motifs could fit. Is there a single issue common to all? Or do the tales give expression to more than one basic issue? Do the motifs suggest a number of ways for resolving a single basic issue?

This is how themes from folktales can be related to biographical themes—with respect to childhood on the one hand, and with respect to one's current passage in life on the other. The aim of this work is to deepen understanding of the self, to define factors that create obstacles, and to increase our effectiveness in dealing with life. It is an illusion to think that we can do away with all of our problems, but it is helpful to identify problem areas and possible ways for coping with them.

Sometimes it is possible to find all the motifs that one remembers in a single folktale. This is different from merely a favorite folktale; it is a tale for one's present life. I do not think that a single folktale can ever give an image for the entire mythological blueprint of an individual's life. The tales that we find relevant give us insight into the constellations of complexes that our lives are entering at a given time.

Another way of working with individual motifs is to have the client write a new story composed of all the motifs that have been recalled. This will spell out a way for dealing at the present moment with the issues that have been identified. Composing a folktale has a therapeutic value of its own; not only does it stretch our imagination, it also gives it structure. When we write down an imaginative journey, wishes and anxieties take on a shape that is much more definite than in ordinary conversation. The beginning portrays a definite threat, the middle proposes marvelous, transformative events, and the end brings these events to a successful conclusion.

The structure provided by the folktale encourages us to surrender to the free flow of fantasy. This is less threatening than if we were asked to imagine without the help of the narrative structure. The free flow of fantasy increases the availability of psychic energy as well as providing access to deeper layers of consciousness. The folktale gives us a key into a world in which fantastic changes are possible, a glimpse of inner utopias and recesses of hope. Once these inner worlds are unlocked, our self-image rediscovers the freedom to change. We can view the world with different eyes, and take a fresh look at the challenges that stand before us. The swamps of our indecision begin to dry and we begin to take hold of our lives again. The conviction returns that we possess the tools we need to make something happen.

There is a diagnostic as well as a therapeutic value in recalling and working with the folktale motifs of our childhood. Diagnostically, we identify basic issues that have long exercised an influence on our lives. The imaginative act of incorporating these motifs into a new narrative is therapeutic, aiding us in discovering new ways to deal with these issues.

EXAMPLE: ISABEL AND THE SNOW QUEEN

A fifty-one-year-old woman enters therapy with the goal of personal growth. She wants to redefine her goals and identity. She feels that she has been living too much for others. She wants to individuate.

During a phase of therapy in which she recalled no dreams, I asked her if she could tell me her favorite fairy tale, or her favorite childhood fairy tale. This intervention was a response to her desire to find a story that would speak to her present life. She was extremely active, good at handling stress, although her high level of activity caused her often to be torn between different projects. My inquiry was also a response to the need to set a specific goal in therapy. This could be done with the help of a method of working with the psyche that stimulates memory at the same time as it triggers the creative impulse, that enhances recall at the same time it opens prospects for the future.

Isabel, as I shall call her, recalled a number of folktale motifs from her early years, and subsequently plunged with "mad delight" into the world that folktales summoned forth. Following is a transcription of the memories that she recorded on tape:

The most beautiful folktale that comes to mind is "The Snow Queen" by Hans Christian Andersen. The most vivid image of that story for me is Kay in the immense ice palace. I can still see the dome that covers it: it is huge, shining, glistening. The floor is an ice mosaic made of tiles of different shapes and colors. Kay sits in the center of this hall. He is stunned by its magnificence and mirrory splendor. The little girl arrives from some distant place, and with her tears of love gets him out of his dazed state.

I am still moved by the idea that tears of love are worth more than all the splendor of the world. And I always marveled at that little girl who would go halfway around the world to find Kay. The scene where she goes back to the gypsies is still very alive and real to me. She never lets herself get distracted or misled. The scene with the two kids still warms my heart. They lived so close to each other under the eaves of the roof, they could practically reach out and touch. They played by going from house to house through the windows that face out onto the little roof. I see the geraniums in bloom. Then the splinter falls into Kay's little eye, and all of the peace is shattered.

The tale of "The Little Mermaid" is just as vivid and alive to me. This mysterious human figure with a fish's tail. A creature whose capacity for love has her carrying all the pain in her body until she can bear it no longer.

And I still remember the classic Grimms' fairy tales, although I no longer recall who told them to me.

"Snow White and the Seven Dwarfs." I always loved to imagine that little table with the little golden plates. The dwarfs who were all trying to guess what had happened. And I used to love to say, "Who ate from my little plate? Who drank from my little

cup?" I always wondered how a piece of apple could kill somebody. And I always wondered how tripping could dislodge the
apple from her throat. How could she come back to life so easily?

I could not understand how love could be summoned out of a
glass casket. That was surprising, strange, and unreal. The evil
stepmother's punishment frightened me. It was so cruel that she
would have to dance on glowing coals, and yet it seemed a just
punishment. Reward and punishment were always important
themes in my childhood, which is why that seemed so right to
me.

"Sleeping Beauty." I always thought that marvelous hedge of
thorns must be full of roses—red roses. And the fascinating
scene in which even the cook was brought to a standstill just as
he was about to hit his kitchen boy.

We had a saying at home that my father used to try to get me
to shut up and behave: "If you raise your hand against your
father, it will rise again out of the grave." This macabre saying
seems mild to me compared to that strange scene with the cook
and his kitchen boy.

And the story goes on because the prince crawls through the
thorny hedge. At that precise moment everything comes back to
life again.

Here is a marvelous example of the effect that folktale images can
have. A macabre, anxiety-provoking image is associated with a
woman's memory of her father. (The image comes from the tale
"The Naughty Child."[32]) The child sees the image against the back-
drop of a story in which the image changes into something else.
With the certainty that it will go away, she can even enjoy the
image. Images can help make frightening memories less threatening.

"Ali Baba and the Forty Thieves." I think I read the tale later in a
book, but I am not sure anymore. I always used to love the huge
cave where the thieves hid and looked at the jewels they had
stolen. It was so dazzling and yet so cozy, so rich in color and
filled with precious things from all over the world. I thought it
must be marvelous to belong to a secret society that had this col-

lection of valuables kept in a place so far removed from the world that everyone else knew.

I always wished I could have a thousand precious things, especially brightly colored things. I still love bright-colored carpets.

Something else that belonged to this marvelous world was the story of the spirit in the bottle. The thing that I found most fascinating was the way in which the spirit was always able to get back into the bottle. How did it manage to squeeze itself through that narrow bottleneck? How could it change sizes so radically?

It must have had something to do with the incomprehensible, marvelous nature of the spirit and its ability to appear in a misty cloud that evaded comprehension. I always wished I could call on a spirit in a bottle to help me out of difficult situations. I especially wished it would help me by whispering things in my ear during examinations.

After gathering these motifs, I asked Isabel to write a story that included the ones that she felt were most important.

At first Isabel found the task too difficult, a not unusual reaction. When this happens, I explain that the point is not to write the folktale to end all folktales. Once she began, Isabel enjoyed the writing very much. I will take a close look at the tale later.

DISCUSSION OF THE MOTIFS THAT WERE RECALLED

The first motif was the redemption scene from Andersen's "Snow Queen." That motif must have resonated with some issue of present concern to Isabel. Next, Isabel recalled two more scenes from the same tale. Isabel summarized the primary meaning of the story in one sentence: "Tears of love are worth more than all the splendor of the world." The main issue has been defined: love or brilliance? This issue had been important for Isabel as a child, and it is important for Isabel as an adult. I assume that the issue came alive for Isabel when she read the story for herself. It was not something that concerned her parents very much. It may happen that the folktales of our childhood recall to us our parents' most beloved and hackneyed issues. But then this too is important psychological material. Parents convey not only their favorite stories to their children, but also their favorite problems.

Here I would like to provide an abbreviated version of "The Snow Queen"[33] with a few interpretive comments in order to examine more closely the themes that arose in my work with Isabel.

THE STORY (summary)

The devils invent a "demonic mirror" that enlarges everything bad and ugly in the world, and makes everything that is good and beautiful smaller. When the goblins try to fly with it up into the sky, it sneers so intensely that they have to let go of it. When it hits the ground, it shatters into a billion tiny pieces. Every shard that falls through the sky has the power of the entire mirror. Splinters fall into people's eyes and hearts. When this happens, they see everything negatively, and their hearts turn to blocks of ice.

Gerda and Kay live just across from each other under the eaves of the rooftops. Their niches are connected by an arching rose vine. Life is like a dream until Kay is struck by one of the splinters. Suddenly he sees what is wrong with everything—except for the snowflakes, whose only fault seems to be that they melt. One day while playing in the snow he is abducted by the Snow Queen. She kisses him to harden his heart and make him forget everyone he might otherwise miss.

When the spring comes, Gerda goes looking for Kay. She lets herself be carried off by a river that brings her to a wonderful garden. A woman lives there to whom Gerda tells her story, after which she makes all the roses sink into the ground so Gerda won't think about Kay. But when she sees a rose painted on the woman's sun hat, she becomes restless again and continues on her journey. Along the way, a crow informs her that Kay lives in a palace and has become very wise. Gerda does not doubt that Kay may have become wise, but she can hardly believe he lives in a palace. After being dressed by a princess in elegant gowns, Gerda is abducted by robbers. A young girl from among the band of thieves saves her from being murdered, in order to win her as a playmate.

After hearing Gerda's story, the little robber girl gives Gerda a reindeer that brings her to the Snow Queen's castle. On their way they stay with a Finn and a Lapp woman who give them help. Finally Gerda arrives at the Snow Queen's castle. In the middle of a vast, snowy hall is a frozen lake that has been shattered into a thousand identically shaped pieces—a work of art. From the middle of the lake, the Snow Queen announces that she is sitting in the mirror of understanding, a mirror that has no parallel in the entire world. And there is Kay, who is blue and on the verge of turning black from the cold, which he does not, however, notice because she "kissed away his icy shiverings." Assembling the shards of ice, he pieces together the mirror of understanding. He plays the "ice game of reason," whose patterns seem to be full of profound significance. But he cannot spell the word "eternity." The Snow Queen had promised him that he could again be his own master and could have the whole world if he could spell that word.

Kay is alone, trying to spell "eternity," when Gerda arrives at the castle. Having banned the icy winds with a prayer, Gerda finds Kay quiet, stiff, and cold, and begins to weep. Her warm tears enter his heart and soften the ice that has hardened it. The song that she sings revives his memory. Kay begins to cry. His tears flow profusely, washing the splinter out of his eye. Now he asks himself, "Where have I been for so long? It is so cold here, so empty." Gerda kisses him, bringing him back to life. Together with the children, the glass shards dance for joy. When they get tired, they lie down to spell the word "eternity." Kay now has his ticket to freedom, and returns home with Gerda. On their way they meet the robber girl. Kay interviews her with the hope of finding out whether the journey that Gerda undertook would be worthwhile for him too. Arriving home, Gerda and Kay realize that they are no longer children, and that they belong together.

In his epic tale, Andersen made use of the well-known "Animal Bridegroom" tale type, especially the motif of the journey of a woman to liberate him from the curse that prevented him from finding his way back to his original love for her. The Grimms' tale "The Lilting, Leaping Lark"[34] is a famous example of this type of tale, which deals with the redemption that a man achieves through a woman and vice versa. Like the heroines of the tales from oral traditions, Gerda goes on a long, dangerous journey, has many adventures, and persists until she finds her Kay. Andersen's story was based on this tradition, but his version is easier to identify with than are the more archaic tales stemming directly from oral traditions.

The story's initial situation shows how "peace is shattered," as Isabel put it. Isabel no longer recalled the image of the devils' mirror, but the idea of peace giving way to danger remained with her as something she had always been afraid of. Idyllic tranquility is disrupted; everywhere she looks she sees only ugliness and injustice. Yet she cannot relinquish her drive for achieving something good and flawless—something brilliant.

The tale suggests that Kay's frozen heart is bound up with a "game of understanding." This is a puzzle that can never be put together. "Eternity" is not something that can be attained through a game of reason; at most it is something that can be experienced in a loving encounter.

The basic message reads: Once we notice what is wrong with things, we can say goodbye to an easy peace of mind; the realm of the demonic can no longer be wished away. At this point we have a choice between playing a cold and theoretical game of understanding—brilliant though it may be—or of going on a "blood and guts" search for what has been lost. Isabel dared to go the way of redemption, convinced that she would find it.

The little robber girl is the most important helper on the way to the palace where Kay is kept on ice. She belongs to a band of murdering thieves, and yet she is kind. Isabel puts her in a good light by calling her a gypsy girl. With an unrefined and refreshing directness, the little robber girl knows how to get what she wants out of

life. Gerda could use more of this, for she is the kind of fairy-tale
heroine who is all too ready to sacrifice everything to win back her
lover. The little robber girl represents the shadow side of someone
like Isabel, who is overprotected. The little robber girl in Isabel is
potentially very dynamic, but has not yet found a strong position in
life.

Isabel will need her gypsy girl—her cruel, yet kind inner thief—
if she is to redeem Kay. She will have to take back possession of a
part of herself that she has repeatedly disowned—throughout her
childhood this part of her was discouraged. And yet the little gypsy
managed to lead a secret underground existence, to Isabel's secret
delight.

Isabel thinks that men get lost in their intellectual games, from
which they need to be rescued and redeemed. Yet her memory of
"The Little Mermaid"[35] leads us to wonder if she is really so sure
this is possible. The little mermaid falls in love with a prince and
saves him from drowning. She has her tail magically transformed
into legs—in spite of knowing that every step she takes will be
painful. If she can win the love of a real man walking on land, she
will come into possession of a living human soul. But she cannot
get the prince to fall in love with her. She is stranded. She would be
allowed to rejoin her family under the sea if she killed her resistant
prince, but she cannot bring herself to sacrifice him, her beloved,
unattainable one.

This tale once again describes a yearning for full human love,
and the willingness to sacrifice everything in order to attain it. But
the mermaid comes much closer than Gerda to witnessing the radical transformation of her love into pain and hatred. The little mermaid is bereft of any sense of belonging; she can neither return to
her underwater family nor make a new home among the people of
land. In the end the daughters of the air in their mercy adopt her.

And what of Isabel's loss of roots? Would she be able to find a
new home and identity for herself? She described the loss of her
peace of mind. Was this a closed chapter of her childhood, or

something that continued to haunt her adult years? The folktale continued to pose questions, making therapy a venture of varied tasks and surprises.

Isabel has of late been enjoying a kind of peace of mind she has never known before: the first truly fulfilling love of her life. And yet there are already some ripples on this calm lake; bound up with this love are intense symbiotic demands. It is not easy to accept the boundaries that continually need to be set. She is worried that the love and peace with herself that she has been enjoying could fall apart. If it does, she knows that she is capable of giving up everything in a desperate attempt to put it back together again. This could end up being very self-destructive. Hello, little mermaid.

What can Isabel's mother complex tell us about Isabel's need for calm? The next motif on her string of folktale recollections is informative. In the tale of "Snow White,"[36] a mother wishes for an extraordinary child. But her daughter makes her extremely envious and resentful that her own beauty has been surpassed. Snow White must run for her life. The seven dwarfs offer her refuge . . .

Snow White finds peace of mind for a time with the seven dwarfs. This is the scene that remained with Isabel. But Snow White is not safe for long; her mother will soon be looking for her. She will attempt to ruin her again and again with her seductive offer of still greater beauty. The mother can be seen as that narcissistic part of Snow White that always has to be more beautiful than all the others. This kind of impossible demand tends to stun us into inactivity. This is the story in the background of Isabel's mother complex. Although Isabel did not mention Snow White's mother, she is necessary in order to explain the importance of the refuge provided by the seven dwarfs.

Like Snow White, Isabel was searching for a new home. In therapy she told me that she was continually on the lookout for mother substitutes. And she found them, which suggests that her earliest bonds to her mother were strong enough. Snow White's mother began to hound her when she was seven. Isabel was slightly older when her mother began competing with her. Her mother refused to allow Isabel to be a person in her own right, misusing her as a mirror of her own self-esteem. Too many demands were made on Isabel, and these demands became a part of her inner psychology, part of her mother complex. Isabel's sense of self-assurance was disrupted by the debilitating effect of these inner demands. At times she could hardly do anything for herself, like Snow White in the glass coffin. She found herself waiting for the enlivening love of a mysterious stranger that would lift her out of her hundred-year sleep. Love seems to be the only way to lift the lid of the coffin into which we collapse when we are overrun by narcissistic demands.

Isabel was daunted by the punishment that was meted out to Snow White's mother, although she recognized that she not only wanted to escape from her mother, but also had a certain desire for revenge. Both of these desires made her feel guilty, and this guilt could well have nagged her into becoming a "good" daughter. But in Isabel's case, the problem was more that the conflict that this created prevented her getting what she needed. Rather than giving her the capacity to nurture herself, the mother within her exercised a poisonously critical influence over her that often paralyzed her completely.

The next motif that came to mind in relation to inactivity was "Sleeping Beauty" or "Briar Rose."[37] In the scene that Isabel found so memorable, everyone falls asleep in the midst of their activities. With a hint of glee, Isabel remembers how the cook is stopped dead in his tracks. Was the kitchen the place where Isabel's father had punished her for her misbehavior? The image helped her overcome repression that blocked memories of being beaten, and it helped her find her way to rage.

Something has gone wrong in the relationship between the king and the queen in "Sleeping Beauty." Their marriage is lacking the blessing that would lead to the birth of a child. Both the king and the queen wanted to pretend that they could avoid reckoning with the dark and demonic side of life. Taking revenge for this neglect, the thirteenth, "forgotten" fairy puts a curse on the girl, that she will die on her fifteenth birthday. But then the twelfth fairy reduces the curse: rather than dying, she will sleep for a hundred years—along with the rest of the court. Sleeping Beauty's father, who plays a leading role in the story, would like to prevent the fulfillment of the prophecy and protect his daughter from her fate, but of course he is powerless to do so.

What can this scenario tell us about Isabel's experiences with her father? In addition to her mother's narcissistic demands and an inhibiting mother complex, Isabel's father also blunted her raw energy in his attempts to tame her wild spirit. Both mother and father had a dulling effect on Isabel—each for his or her own reason—which could only be countered by the cultivation of a free spirit. The robber girl offers a concise image of what is needed.

Thinking more about the roses than the thorns, Isabel is hopeful about the possibility of transformation and redemption. A loving prince can set her back into motion. But the strength of this hope needn't wash away the blackness of the curse. It won't be too easy to get through this hedge of thorns, especially if entry is attempted before the hundred years of solitude is up.

But in Isabel's memory, the prince does penetrate the thorny wall, bringing everything back to life again. From here she moves to the rich and mysterious cave from "Ali Baba and the Forty Thieves"[38] in *1001 Nights*, specifically the scene in which Ali Baba takes delight in the treasures the robbers have gathered.

When Ali Baba saw that the door was open, he entered and closed it behind him. And when he remembered the saying "Open Sesame," he was no longer afraid. "It doesn't matter if the door closes again," he told himself. "I know the secret saying that will make it open again." Expecting the cave to be dark, he was amazed when he came to a grand, brightly lit hall made of marble, lined with sumptuous pillars, and filled with every kind of food and drink the heart could possibly desire. From there he went into a second hall that was even larger and grander than the first. There he saw marvelous things, gems that sparkled and dazzled the senses, bars of gold, genuine and pure, and other fine wares of silver, coins of various sizes all heaped up like piles of pebbles and sand, far too many to count. After gazing a while into this marvelous hall, another door opened before him. He went through it and came into yet a third hall, even more majestic and beautiful than the second. It was filled with the finest garments from every land on the face of the earth, made of fine cotton, silk, and the most magnificent brocades of the world. Every kind of sumptuous fabric was to be found there, from Syria, Africa, China, India, Nubia, and Ceylon. From there he went into the hall of precious gems. This was the largest and most wonderful of all. There were pearls and jewels, too many to take in or count, sapphires and emeralds, turquoise and topaz. There were piles of pearl, agate, and coral. Finally he entered the last hall, the room of the most delicate and fine incense, spice, and perfume. The fragrance of aloe wood and musk rose up, ambergris and myrrh wafted majestically forth, the magic of rosewater and nard (a perfume from ambergris, musk, and aloe wood) filled the air, incense and saffron rose marvelously forth. Bits of sandalwood lay about ready to be burned. Aromatic roots had been strewn about without the least concern for their value. Ali Baba was blinded by the sight of these immeasurable treasures. His senses were dazzled. Dazed and completely overcome, he just stood there awhile. . . .

Following Isabel's winding way through her memorial garden of folktale motifs, we have arrived at a secret storehouse of treasures and valuables, a place to revel in the beauty of all the marvelous things the world has to offer, to wonder at the never-ending plenty and color of life.

Where is this cave of treasure to be located in Isabel's biography? Was it a thing of her past, of her future? It is revealing that Isabel has recalled a part of the story in which Ali Baba himself becomes a thief. With the help of a very clever maid, he tricks all of the robbers, one after the other, until it all belongs to him. Shady figures who cannot withstand the light of day gather up the valuables—a nice illustration of the riches lying hidden in the shadow. This scene had lost none of its appeal for Isabel. But Isabel was not yet up to following Ali Baba's example by outwitting the robbers and integrating the riches that they had gathered into her life.

At this point she was still busy taking delight in her newly discovered inner wealth, and her secret identity with a clan of thieves that would stick together come hell or high water. It was not yet time for the robbers to enter the light of her consciousness. For now, they were content to stay in the dimly lit corners of her underground caves.

In the figure of the little robber girl, we already met a pocket of Isabel's secret of forbidden wealth. Now we see her potential inner wealth in more sumptuous detail. The thief in Isabel is a part of her will to fight and take what it wants, with little or no concern for propriety.

The motifs that Isabel recalled have acquainted us with a number of forms and transformations of her drive for self-assertion: thievish delight in assembling goods to please her senses ("Ali Baba and the Forty Thieves"); invincible stamina in pursuing a goal that leads to redemption ("The Snow Queen"); narcissistic demands that paralyze the will ("Snow White," "Sleeping Beauty").

Isabel's fascination with her secret inner world took her down a path that led into a cave of hoarded riches and through the neck of a bottle where she caught a glimpse of the mystery of the spirit itself. The last story that she recalled was the "The Spirit in the Bottle."[39]

A woodcutter wanted to send his son to school, but he didn't have any more money. So the son came back home and asked his father for work cutting wood. While he was taking a break, he found a bottle. In the bottle was a spirit. "Let me out," begged the spirit. The student opened the bottle. When it came out, the spirit pumped itself up like a balloon until it towered over him, and announced that he was the great Mercurius who would have to snuff out the woodcutter's son. But the student had his wits about him, and challenged the spirit to prove that he was really the great Mercurius. If it was true that he had been sitting in the bottle, he should be able to enter again. That was easy enough for the spirit, and once he was back inside the student wasted no time in corking the bottle. "Let me out," said the spirit, begging the student, promising him vast riches. The student took a chance, and let the spirit out again. He gave the student a cloth, one side of which would heal any wound, the other side of which would make silver out of iron. The student tried it out, and it worked. He became the most famous doctor in the world.

Isabel had forgotten the ending of the story, which would have been interesting for her to recall since she too had become a doctor. There were other points of contact between the story and Isabel's biography as well. For instance, Isabel had earned money for her studies by splitting wood. The most memorable thing about the story for Isabel was the marvel of the expansive spirit. She felt that her studies had acquainted her with this spirit, even if only for the mundane purpose of helping her finish her assignments.

The last two stories bring us into realms that have a very different feel from those at the beginning. From out of the mist, new colors appear in the rainbow of Isabel's personality. Suddenly there are hidden riches and secret helpers. The mood changes to a fascination with the abundance of things, with the marvel of the spirit.

But was all this anything more than a medley of folktale motifs? What concrete therapeutic gains did Isabel make by remembering and bringing them into a more coherent whole?

First, Isabel learned more about a destructive aspect of her father complex. The mirror that reflects what is wrong about everything made her think of her father. His life seemed to be haunted by the negative glimmerings of imperfection at every turn. Finding fault with everyone else, it is no wonder that he became quite lonely. Isabel had gone out of her way to live a life that was diametrically opposed to this. Seeing the silver lining in every cloud, she felt blessed by the gleam of goodness almost everywhere she looked.

And yet when she looked at herself, she seemed quite ready to see herself through her father's dark spectacles. Her vision of herself was twisted by a mirror that distorted things so badly that she sometimes saw only her shortcomings. With this self-punishing attitude, she would mete out to herself cold and stiff judgments. Somewhere, out of reach of this poisonous mirror, was the "Gerda" part of herself, whose hope for love and life remained intact. Isabel saw that she could be like Gerda and like Kay.

When she was like Kay, she had a splinter in her eye, and her love life would take a sudden turn for the worse. She would put herself down, and her partner would try to lift her up and put her back on her feet. In the process, he brought himself down too. Why was he in love with someone who was so hard on herself? He would retreat into his mind games, and her peace of mind was destroyed. It took quite some time for her to catch on to what the "devils' mirror" was doing to her. The remedy was for her to call on the "Gerda" part of herself, with whose help she could remobilize her positive energies.

Another therapeutic gain was a greater capacity to surrender to the sensual joy that beautiful objects gave her. The image of Ali Baba in the cave of glittering treasures helped her to see beyond the purely materialistic side of her desire for plenty, riches, and color. She had a hard time convincing herself that her craving for beautiful material things was only the surface of a deeper desire for beauty itself. She wondered if her craving was really greedy and covetous, no better than that of the band of robbers. She had a tendency to judge the pleasure she took in things as "stolen" rather than earned. Her mother complex intensified her need to have nice things at the same time as it deprived her of the capacity to enjoy them. The secret pleasure that she took in the stolen riches of Ali Baba's cave helped free her imagination from this judgmentalism.

Finally, Isabel's effort to recall and reorganize her memories of folktale motifs called her to a quest for transcendence. She could hardly believe that she had forgotten about the scene from "The

Snow Queen" where Kay tries to spell the word *eternity*. This elusive word seemed like the solution to the riddle of her life. Her romance gave her a sense of things working from behind the scenes. Hidden meanings came alive. Sometimes a single moment seemed to last forever. She described her intimation of eternity as "freedom from the Snow Queen and the pain of things passing, freedom for which we fight, freedom for which we love."

ISABEL'S ORIGINAL FOLKTALE

One way to continue working with the motifs that Isabel recalled would have been to encourage her to adapt a traditional folktale to her personal situation. The Grimms' tale "The Lilting, Leaping Lark" would have lent itself to this task, since it contains many of Isabel's motifs, but it would have left out several crucial ones. Or we could have entered into a more detailed examination of the motifs that she had recalled. In the end, I invited her to compose her own folktale out of the most important motifs. This is what she wrote:

Wondrous Tears
In a small medieval town there lived two children, Isabel and Kay. They didn't live in the same house, but the streets of this little town were so narrow that the houses practically touched each other. The balconies on the first floor almost touched each other as well, so that the children could go from balcony to balcony to talk and play.

One beautiful summer day, when all the flowers on the balconies were in vibrant bloom, the children were having fun playing together. They were still too young for school, and they had no chores, so they could simply enjoy the summer day.

All of a sudden Kay yelped, "Ouch! A splinter fell in my eye. Where did it come from? Can you see it, Isabel? Help! My eye hurts so bad! I can hardly see a thing!" Isabel looked at his eye, but she couldn't see anything—no splinter, nothing. And there was nothing to see, since the splinter was of ice, which the children couldn't have known.

Kay's eye started to feel better, and since Isabel still couldn't see anything, Kay became increasingly angry and told her she was stupid for not being able to find anything. Suddenly he left her alone and went inside. Isabel protested that there really was nothing to be seen. Why was Kay so mad? Why did he leave? Nothing like that had ever happened before.

For the next few days Isabel went out onto the balcony at the usual time and called out for Kay. Kay didn't appear, although the sun was shining and the summer was as pleasant as ever. Isabel could not find where he was hiding. One day she left home. After wandering through the narrow streets, she left the village and went on a journey to find Kay. She asked plants, animals, and people if they had seen her Kay. Wandering through the country, she was continually surprised by how vast everything was. She forgot about her loneliness. But she continued to ask everyone if they had seen Kay, without any luck. She kept on going without any plan in mind. Gradually she began to grow frightened and felt alone.

Then she came to a gypsy camp. She gazed at the many people and children all dressed in bright colors. Everyone was so busy. There was a large fireplace where the evening meal was being cooked. The aroma of meat on the spit wafted seductively toward her. Hunger overcame her. Happy that she was no longer alone, she made her way into the colorful crowd. The children were glad to have someone new to play with. No one asked her where she had come from or where she was going. She even forgot to ask if they had seen Kay.

There was no question of being adopted by the group. With so many kids, one more was hardly noticed. When evening came and the temperature dropped, she went with the other gypsies into a large cave in the hillside where they made their beds. The glow of oil lamps and torches in various corners filled the caves with a mysterious light. Copper lamps and silver lanterns added their shimmering brilliance. Bright carpets hung on the walls. The atmosphere was exotic and magical.

Feeling cozy, Isabel lay down with the others to sleep. When she awoke the next morning, she forgot all about her search for Kay. She was entranced by the thousand precious and wonderful things to admire. Feeling at peace, she stayed. The gypsies took her with them everywhere they went. Together they wandered on long journeys throughout the world. Isabel saw foreign landscapes, magnificent forests, huge lakes. She enjoyed getting to know all the beautiful things of the world, and grew even fonder of returning to the large cave in which she kept discovering new valuables that the gypsies brought back from their distant travels.

With time she grew into a tall and charming young lady. Sometimes when she sat in front of the cave and watched the sun go down, she felt a dull pain in her heart, she didn't know why. Sometimes she had a clue, as if something were there to remember, but she could not think of what it was. And then the other young folks came and danced, and she forgot about it again.

One fine evening the gypsies were visited by some mysterious foreign men of dark complexion who had come from afar. They asked for lodging, and after they had eaten and drunk, and had been asked about where they had come from and where they were going, they performed acrobatics and magic tricks. Everyone was delighted. The gypsies knew a few tricks themselves—how else would they have been able to return from their travels with such booty? But what they now witnessed was beyond them.

One of the visitors, an especially gifted magician, was clearly the leader. After all the others were finished, he said he had something special he wanted to show them. Out of his back he took a bottle with a large belly and a narrow neck that was closed with a special latch. "In this bottle," he announced, "is a big spirit that belongs to me. If I say the magic word, he can come out of the bottle. If I am able to say another magic word and get him to cooperate, he will grant me any wish I like, except for things like gold and jewels." No one believed him. But he showed them that it was true.

With mysterious, incomprehensible sayings and movements he uncorked the bottle. At first only a thin white wisp of smoke left the neck of the bottle. But then it grew larger and larger, and took on a superhuman, fantastic shape. The magician continued his invocation. "Spirit," he called out. "What do you see here among these people that we don't see? Can you bring us something special?" The ghostly shape swayed to and fro for a long time, and then spoke with a deep, echoing voice. "There is among you a girl who has come a great distance—no one knows from where. She still has a long way to go. No one here knows what her destination will be, but she will find her way. On her way she will stop in the large city, where she will attend a special school. There she will learn all she needs to know in order to invoke me some day, and ask me favors." Before the gypsies could look around to see whom the spirit was speaking of, the huge shape twisted itself back into a thin wisp of smoke and sucked itself back into the bottle, which the magician corked and latched.

Suddenly everyone realized whom the spirit had been speaking of. They now knew that Isabel had come from afar, and that she still had a long way to go. Suddenly they treated her like a foreigner who didn't really belong there. They went to great pains to equip her with everything she would need for her long journey. She would leave the very next day. There was great hustle and bustle until late at night in the camp of the gypsies.

One person was sad, and did not take part in any of the preparations: a gypsy boy, unremarkable except the darkness of his eyes. He carefully observed all of the preparations, watching everything the girl did. When everyone had quieted down again, including the girl, he approached her in private to wish her well on her travels. There were tears in his eyes. As if by magic, the girl felt suddenly drawn to him as to an old friend. She took him by the hand, tried to comfort him, kissed him, and told him she would come back again. The young fellow responded passionately when she kissed him, and she was deeply shocked to think again of Kay. In her mind's eye she saw Kay sitting in a bright and magnificent palace of ice crystals. She saw him, alone under the broad dome, staring into space and at the patterns of ice on the floor as if in a mirror. Now Isabel knew where her travels would take her. She must find Kay. She must rescue him. This was what she had not been able to remember. This was what caused such pain in her heart.

She stroked the gypsy youth's hair one last time, lifted the bags that had been made ready, and left the gypsy camp in the middle of the night.

She knew now that it was the Snow Queen who had put a curse on Kay with the splinter of ice. She knew now that she would be able to save him from it. She wandered through the world, day in and day out, until she came to a big city with a large school. Just as the spirit said, she attended the school and learned everything she could. She knew she would need this knowledge if she was going to do what she had to do. She no longer forgot about Kay. She knew the reason for her pain. She could still see her vision of Kay in the vast hall of the ice palace.

Once she had learned everything the school had to offer, and she felt certain that she would be able to invoke the spirit if she needed to, she went on her way. No longer did she ask anyone if they had seen Kay. She found the way herself to the Snow Queen's imposing palace, with its thousand towers and glistening ornaments. There she invoked the spirit and commanded his assistance in finding her way through the labyrinth of ice. Without becoming visible, the spirit guided her through many side halls until she came to the central hall of the dome. There she saw Kay, a wonderfully handsome young man with distant eyes, sitting in the middle of the hall—just as she had seen him in her visions.

The minute she recognized him, she ran up to him and threw her arms around him, looked deep in his eyes, and kissed him. He showed no reaction. He seemed not to recognize her. With anguish and tears she pressed him close. "Kay, Kay, it's Isabel!" Warm tears ran down her face and onto Kay's face and into his eyes, dislodging the splinter of ice. Suddenly he could see everything clearly. He knew now that it was Isabel who had come for him. He felt her love, looked deep into her eyes, and kissed her. Hand in hand, they left the palace of ice. They were bound in love, and the Snow Queen's magic could no longer touch them.

The story portrays the redemption of a cursed lover—psychologically, the redemption of an inner, repressed, masculine part of the personality. The journey that Isabel described in her folktale for reaching this redemption is a process of psychic growth. It is a way to greater personal freedom, but also a way to a deeper relationship, a path that is indicated for many people who suffer from the kind of estrangement that befalls Kay and Isabel at the beginning of the tale.

The Snow Queen poses a threat, and the danger lies in her magic. But the magic of this icy, marvelous brilliance is dangerous only to those who are not bound in love. The curse has no effect on those who are. The Snow Queen rules by her icy mind games, by the tyranny of perfection, and the elimination of error, emotion, and warmth. Isabel came under the thumb of the Snow Queen through her relationship to her father, who attempted to cleanse her of all that was emotional and unruly. The Snow Queen is an image for the tendency to avoid feeling in order to see things clearly. The Snow Queen reminds us of the devils' mirror, which Isabel mentioned just before beginning her story. This mirror was a dark glass that saw everything that is wrong. Part of the fascination of perfection is the sense of being able to identify the fault in everything. In Isabel's life, it was primarily her father who represented this side. An animus figure whom she calls Kay has been fixated by the Snow Queen's power.

Reviewing the story that she wrote, Isabel saw each part of the story as a phase of her life—something she had not intended before writing the story. The stay with the gypsies was the time of her youth, when she belonged to various groups, enjoyed a great deal of togetherness, and felt calm. The encounter with the spirit was the time of her studies. She wanted to know something about the spirit, to enter the halls of her intellect. The next phase was that of relationship. Isabel described the journey of a woman with a father complex, a woman who moves through the world of the spirit and intellect before moving into the world of committed relationships.

Let us examine this process more carefully. Isabel's story begins with the pain of separation, and her travels end with the achievement of redemption and rapprochement.

Her adoption by the band of child gypsies fills the gap in psychic development that she needed in order to go on to redeem Kay. Here she was able to live out her childlike, gypsy self, the part of her that was slightly thievish. Here she discovers the peace of mind and sense of belonging that she did not get at home. Here in the shadow of her childhood she experiences a simple profundity. This extended family gives her a social womb in which a branch of her personality can grow that will give her the strength to begin to integrate her shadow.

The stay with the gypsies is only a transitional phase. A subtle pain in her heart reminds her that yet more is required before she can still her longing. The spirit is like a guiding paternal hand that instructs her in what to do next. When the time comes, the spirit orders her to leave the nurturing community and go on to the next task. Now she becomes more deeply involved with the spirit, and is even promised that some day she will be able to gain the spirit's cooperation in reaching her own personal goals.

Before entering the halls of the spirit, she has an intimate encounter with a gypsy youth that pricks her conscience and reminds her of the decision she made to redeem Kay. With this love rekindled in her heart, she is calm again, and receptive enough to learn the ways of the spirit. Her description of putting the spirit to work seems a bit facile. Perhaps at some later point she will make another apprenticeship. But for now Isabel has learned enough, and she finds her way to Kay. The curse is undone when she shows him her grief and risks complete rejection.

Isabel wrote her life as a folktale—a life that is never exempt from the danger of getting caught in stultifying mind games, a life that is never free from a twisted attitude in which everything seems wrong, unattractive, and on the verge of dying, a life that is always dependent on someone else's feeling responses and soul-searching to find out why things have reached the freezing point. Isabel and Kay represent two sides of her personality. When they come together they make for a feeling of love, wholeness, and happiness.[40] But this inner couple is always threatened with separation. To find Kay again, Isabel must continually take the role of Isabel in her story, who goes in search of Kay.

The motifs from the stories of "Snow White," "Sleeping Beauty," and "The Little Mermaid" have receded somewhat. These childhood themes represent the background of her present issues, but they no longer occupy center stage. At the time of the writing of this story, Isabel felt that the character of Isabel represented the attitude of emotional decisiveness that she had adopted.

TO WRITE A FOLKTALE

Isabel felt satisfied to have written her own folktale. She felt as if she had been able to conjure a small spirit out of the bottle.

The story helped her see around the corners of her problems into the secret doorways of her inner riches. She no longer felt as powerless to counter the problems that were ruling her life. She had a greater sense of freedom in being able to shape things more to her liking.

This kind of experience is typical when writing an original folktale, provided one's expectations are not too high. In the process of composing one's own story, problematical themes tend to lead to new strategies. Many people become aware of their creative potential for the first time. Creativity tends to stimulate motivation to change and unlock the psychic energy that works major transformations.

Recovering and reworking motifs from the folktales of childhood contributed to a process of centering such as one would hope therapy might provide. Questions were posed of Isabel that might not otherwise have been arisen.

Folktales intensified the therapeutic process. Isabel felt the folktale coming to her as a kind of gift. And the tale was a gift for me as well. Isabel's self-esteem was enhanced in the giving of this gift. Her joy was further enhanced when I asked her if I might use her materials for lectures and publications. This deepened the significance of her work. She was accustomed to having success in her career, but it was new for her to have such success with a folktale.

BELOVED ROLAND

Group Work with Folktales

Group work with folktales is a kind of interpersonal encounter mediated by an "object." Without having to talk directly about one-self, one shares quite a bit. We speak to each other's story images without having to say what we think outright. We talk to each other indirectly. The folktale acts as a many-faceted transitional object.

The folktale suggests a "next step" that a process of emotional growth might take, without insisting on its literally taking place. The tale—either as a whole or in its individual motifs—creates a space in which to reflect on oneself, giving rise to insights and hints for how to change one's life. The mirror of folktales offers insight into one's problems in a narcissistically protective wrapping. The problem can be worked on in its projection on the motif. The image helps one find words for one's motifs to trigger one's own images, after which they drop into the background. This freedom is typical of work with folktales—in groups and in general.

Folktales are one step further away from our emotional experi-ence than dreams, for which we are more likely to feel personally responsible. But folktales are hardly so distant that we are emotion-ally immune to them. Conducive to the creative process, folktales provide an open, nonthreatening space for emotions to do their work.

In what follows I will describe the work on a folktale that was undertaken by a group during a workshop on the theme of "anxiety." We worked as a group on the tale for five sessions of three hours each. I chose the tale on account of its portrayal of courage winning out over anxiety, and the transformation of danger through renewal. Presenting a folktale to a group that is concerned with a specific issue gives a particular framing to that issue. It also imbues that issue with the hope—typical of folktales—that a solution will be found.

THE STORY[41]

There was once a woman who was a real witch. She had two daughters. One of them, who was ugly and bad, was her own daughter. The other, her stepdaughter, was beautiful and good. She liked her own daughter much more, and hated the other, since she was a stepdaughter. Now the stepdaughter had a very pretty apron that her stepsister was very fond of, and coveted. So she told her mother, "I want that apron." "That's all you need to say, my dear," said the old woman. "You'll have your apron. Your stepsister has long since outlived her lease on life. Tonight when she's sleeping, I'll hack her head off. Go to sleep now, and make sure she takes the place at the outer edge of the bed." That would have been the end of the good little girl if she had not been standing quietly in the corner listening to everything they said. When it was time to go to bed, the good sister let the bad sister go to bed first so she could sleep where she wanted. Once her sister had fallen asleep, she pushed her to the outer edge of the bed and lay down next to the wall.

Late that night their mother sneaked into their room. She had the axe in her right hand. With her left hand she felt around to see if there was someone sleeping at the outer edge of the bed. Then she took the axe with both hands and hacked off the head of her own daughter.

When the witch was gone, the good girl went straight to her beloved Roland and knocked on his door. "Listen, Roland," she said to him as he opened the door, "we have to get out of here right away. My stepmother just tried to kill me, but she killed her own daughter instead. When she wakes up in the morning, she will see what she has done, and it will be the end of us." Roland said, "First we have to steal her magic wand so we can get away when she comes after us." The girl went and fetched the magic wand. Then they took the severed head and let three drops of blood fall: one on the floor by the bed, one in the kitchen, and one on the stairs leading up to the front door. Then they left together.

The next morning when the witch got up, she called her daughter to give her the apron. There was no answer. "Where are you?" she called out. "Over here on the stairs," said the first drop of blood. She went outside, but she couldn't find anyone on the stairs. "Where are you?" "I'm in the kitchen warming myself up by the stove," said the second drop of blood. But the old woman couldn't find anyone in the kitchen either. "Where are you?" "I'm in bed, sleeping," called out the third drop of blood. When the witch went into the bedroom she saw it: her own child swimming in a pool of blood. She herself had hacked off the head.

Flying into a rage, she went straight to the window. With her supersharp eyes she spotted her stepdaughter making her getaway with her beloved Roland. "You think you're fancy free," she cackled, "but you'll be mine before you know it." With her seven-league boots on, it took only a few steps to catch up with them. But the girl knew what was coming, and with the help of the magic wand she turned Roland into a pond and herself into a duck swimming across the surface. The witch sat down at the edge of the pond and tried everything she could think of to get the duck to swim over to her. When even bread crumbs floating on the water couldn't get the duck to come, the old woman had to go home empty-handed. That evening, as soon as she was gone, the pond and the duck turned back into man and woman, which made it easier to enjoy the night together. At the break of dawn the girl turned into a pretty flower growing in the middle of a thorny hedge and Roland turned into a fiddle player. Soon the witch was back again. "Would you mind, dear fiddler," she asked, "if I picked that nice flower?" "Not at all." he replied, "I will even play a little tune to help you." Without waiting another minute, she crawled into the hedge and lunged for the flower. She knew who the flower was. When the fiddler began to play, the magic of the music made her dance like a marionette. He didn't stop playing until the thorns of that hedge had ripped off her clothes and had pricked and scratched her so that she bled to death.

As soon as they were saved from the witch, Roland announced, "I'm going to tell my father that we are getting married." "I'll stay here and wait for you," said the girl. "In the meantime, I don't want anyone to see me, so I'll turn myself into a red stone." Roland left, and the girl—now a red stone—waited for her beloved. Once Roland was home again, another girl managed to make him forget all of his promises. Roland's true beloved stood there for a long time waiting for him to return. When she finally realized that he was not coming back, she turned into a very sad flower, who thought to herself, "Someone will probably come along and step on me."

But as it happened, a shepherd discovered the flower. He couldn't just leave that flower behind. "Never in my life have I seen such a beautiful flower," he exclaimed as he put her safely in his cabinet. From then on the shepherd's household was graced with good luck. When he got up in the morning, all the housework had already been done. The living room had been cleaned and organized, the fire was burning, the water had been drawn. At midday when he came home, the table was set and a fine meal was waiting for him. He had no idea how it all came about, for he never saw anyone in his house. In the beginning he was delighted, but after a while it began to make him nervous, so he went to consult a wise old woman. "There's magic at work," she warned him. "Take a good look early in the morning and see what's going on in the living room. If you see anything move, throw a white cloth over it. That will stop the magic." The shepherd did as he was instructed. The next morning he saw the cabinet door opening and the flower coming out. He dashed right over and threw a white cloth over it. That ended the magic, and suddenly there was a beautiful girl standing in front of him.

Now he knew who had been doing his housework. He thought she was so beautiful he wanted to marry her. But she refused, *because she wanted to remain faithful to her beloved Roland. So she compromised and agreed to stay with him and keep house for him.*

Some time later Roland's wedding was publicly announced. There was a custom that all single girls should go and line up to sing in honor of the bride. When Roland's first love heard that he was getting married to another woman, her heart was broken. She had no desire to attend the wedding, but she had no choice. When it was her turn to sing, she could not, and went to the back of the line again. But when in the end she did sing, Roland was so moved that he leaped to his feet and called out, "This is my true bride. I will have no other." He had recognized her voice immediately, and suddenly everything about her came back to his heart. The girl married her beloved Roland. Her pain was over, her happiness just beginning.

THE WORK

PART ONE

After a few relaxation exercises, the tale is read to the group. Participants are invited to imagine the story as vividly as possible. After the reading, they are asked to review the images they experienced and single out those that had the greatest impact, positively or negatively. Often the same image has both valences.

If the group is not too large (up to fifteen), it is often a good idea to follow this first encounter with the tale with a round of introductions in which the participants introduce themselves by sharing those images that concerned them the most, or by telling the passage that most impressed or angered them.

Of course no one is compelled to say more than they want to at any time during the meeting.

This particular group consisted of fifteen participants: nine women and six men. The youngest person was thirty-two, the oldest seventy-five. In the round of introductions it became apparent that most of the key passages of the tale had struck a chord in the imaginations of the participants. Fleshed out with personal fantasies and associations, the images had already touched on issues of everyday life. But it also became apparent that certain passages from the tale had been skipped over or avoided. For instance, no one cared to deal with the beginning of the tale. Since the tale had to be taken as a whole, we decided to try to act out the beginning.

The technique that was used was similar to the "dramatic play" of psychodrama, in which various members of the group act out different parts. Taking the initial scene from the tale, the action is allowed to depart from the text if it seems to be going in that direction. This freedom can be especially helpful for participants who are not used to allowing themselves a flexible space for play.

Each player should play as many parts as possible from a particular scene, a rule that applies to interpretation on the subjective level. Thus, in the initial scene each person should have a turn at playing the witch, the ugly daughter, and the beautiful daughter. Men and women play both masculine and feminine roles.

The first scene evoked the theme of sibling rivalry, and of envious mothers and fathers. What happens when one child is favored over another? Perhaps one child receives less attention because she has more difficulties. Less attention increases her difficulties. Then there is the mother's envy of the advantages that her daughter has over her. The problem of envy is illuminated by a wide variety of perspectives provided by participants of various age groups.

Ways of dealing with envy that are less productive also enter the discussion. One way is to eliminate the person who is envied. Symbolically, this can be seen as a denial of someone's existence, in the hope that the thing that causes such envy might become the possession of the person who feels envious. Here it is the pretty apron— an image of bliss—that causes such envy. Most of us are familiar with the fantasy. Death would do away with the envied person once and for all, but the qualities that he possesses are not so easily transferable. In fact, the impetus to develop them in oneself are much greater as long as the person is alive.

In the tale, the fight erupts over the apron. But it is clear that this apron is more than an apron: it has a certain sex appeal. Those who put it on attract the attention of male admirers. In our playacting, the part of the flirtatious young girl was played by a man.

Like the womb, the apron symbolizes a protective space.[42] But the apron not only protects, it also advertises. The good girl in this tale announces with her apron that she is looking for a man. The apron could also symbolize the unspoiled times from her past, although these were not mentioned in the tale. Maybe her father or her mother gave her the apron. Maybe she got it at a time when she still had a mutually loving relationship with her mother.

The Brothers Grimm often replaced the real mother with the figure of an evil stepmother with the aim of encouraging children in their struggles for greater personal autonomy.

There are no men at the beginning of this tale, however. Relationships with men seem to be uneasy. The story concerns itself with the building of a relationship. At the beginning we are confronted with a complete witch of a mother. She plans to kill the daughter who still has a measure of happiness, the daughter who is going to separate from her and leave home. She will put her own daughter in her place. She behaves destructively from the outset. As it progresses, the tale describes a process of growth that allows for partnership and for personal wholeness, all of which takes place against the background of the destructive, enslaving power of a negative mother complex.

This interpretation emerged naturally from the playacting, which allows for a reflective response to an emotional reaction. In our dramatic enactment, the apron was the coveted object. It seemed to guarantee happiness. But neither mother nor daughter wanted to take responsibility for her possessiveness. No one wanted to be bad.

There is an important lesson here that extends beyond the tale itself. It is easy to talk and think about evil. Few of us raise many objections to the fruits of necessary evil, and most of us are quite ready to allow someone else to do the dirty work for us. Folktale enactments give rise to such experiences again and again, bringing us face to face with the disparity between our beliefs and our behavior.

Understandably enough, no one cared to enact the murder scene. This scene should be understood symbolically. Encouraging this viewpoint, folktales show us again and again that important things can't be gotten rid of with a single stroke of the axe. The nice daughter just happens to overhear her stepmother's plans. But one thing is certain: If she stays there with her mother and sister, she will remain caught in the attitude that they represent. She will die there. She will not be able to realize the good fortune that comes to her through the apron. She will not grow out of her mother complex. It is necessary for something to be eliminated, to be killed. From the perspective of the stepdaughter, it is the daughter who is closer to the mother who must be eliminated: she who wants to stay in her mother's womb, whose sense of adventure is stifled, who only wishes she could have things that others have, instead of going out on her own.

How might a young woman's life reflect this folktale situation? Let us take a woman who suffers from a strongly negative mother complex. We might imagine that this complex is expressed in her envy, possessiveness, and destructiveness. Her identification with the complex gives her power, but also makes her destructive. She is aware that she has another side that is quite different from this; she is also the "nice stepdaughter with the pretty apron." She knows she has this side of herself that is oriented toward life, nourishing relationships, and things that she finds beautiful. In the language of folktales, "beautiful" suggests good fortune. The positive relationship that she enjoyed with her mother draws this out of her. All of our relationships with our mothers have both positive and negative sides.

The threat of death warns of the danger of stopping this "free" side. The part of her that reacts out of the mother complex could take control. Feelings of greed, destructiveness, and power could completely overshadow those of openness to life, trust, and joy.

Her envious, destructive, greedy side must be sacrificed. She must make a radical departure from this side of herself, while retaining awareness of the danger that it could overtake her again at any moment. She must employ all of the energy that is available to her through her mother complex in order to separate herself from her destructive attitude.

The departure is something she can do only with the help of her beloved Roland. The masculine principle is a typical helper on the way to freedom from symbiotic ties. We think here of growth out of symbiosis in childhood,[43] and of the myth of Demeter and Kore. The masculine principle may take the form of a helper or of a thief (Hades). In "Beloved Roland," he takes the form of a helpful lover.

The folktale portrays the development of the good daughter's relationship with Roland, who could also be seen as the masculine part of herself, the story of a relationship that is girded with a maternal energy that has become ruthless, restrictive, and destructive. Aware of the danger that the witch represents, Roland alerts the good daughter that she needs to get hold of the magic wand; she needs to take hold of her own magical potential. An important bit of wisdom lies in this wand. As unpleasant as they may be, the things that happen to us usually contain hidden lessons for life, strategies for survival, skills for transformation. Thus, children who grow up in difficult circumstances often develop a greater variety of strategies that they can use later in life than children who have had it easier.

The threat, envy, and anxiety at the beginning of the story had a very oppressive effect on the group. They were very glad to be given a magic wand to hold on to at the end of the first session. The wand seemed to promise a way of getting out of the debilitating envy, a way of taking things into one's own hands. It was a symbol of transformation out of a bad situation. The wand encouraged fantasies of coping, in contrast to those of victimization.

I invited the participants to take another break for relaxation, and then to imagine their magic wands, to think of what they would touch and what they would change. At the conclusion of this Imagination came the question of where each person kept his or her magic wand when it was not in use. The idea was to cultivate a capacity for finding the magic wand, since what usually happens is that we can never find it when we need it.

This exercise dramatically changed the group atmosphere. Everyone in the group was pleasantly surprised to find their magic wand. This conveyed the conviction that whatever problems came up could be dealt with. The hope that resides in folktales came alive.

PART TWO

The group members are invited to relax again. I read the part of the tale to them in which the witch flies into a rage when the fleeing lovers turn into a duck and a pond.

The participants are told to immerse themselves in the images and let them do their work. Time is taken to dwell imaginatively on the image that was most vivid, and to allow that image to develop and change. With some people the image develops more according to the logic of the story, with others more according to the personal problem that is brought to the story. We talk about the images that arose. Our comments focus on the tale rather than on ourselves. Then we paint the images that had the most impact on us.

This part of the folktale deals with escaping from the clutches of a destructive maternal energy within oneself. How can one avoid the trap of being swallowed up by an overpowering disabling feeling? In the language of symbols, the story offers a detailed description of how this process of distancing can be accomplished. There must be a severance of the identification with the negative dimension of the mother complex. The first part of this process takes place by avoiding, the second by searching for identity.

The narrative enters here into a "transformation flight," a motif that typically occurs in folktales when the protagonist must avoid a confrontation that he or she can only lose.[44] Psychologically, this means departing from every thought and action that stems from the persecuting figure. The girl in the story cannot afford to allow herself to have envious and destructive feelings. She must indulge in evasive, compulsive behavior, committing herself to the care of others, if necessary, in order to create an alternate space to the one that is so destructive for her.

Even if the transformation flight is a pattern of avoidance, the story suggests that it may well have its merit. At this point in the narrative, it is clear that Roland and his girlfriend have a real relationship. It usually happens that the way a girl gets out of her suffocating relationship with her mother is by means of a lover. This applies to the objective level of outer relationships as much as to the subjective level of inner relationships: when a woman has a relationship to the inner masculine part of herself, she begins to feel a certain completeness. This can help her out of the mother complex's protective zone. Roland, who represents the second element that is necessary for a successful flight, alerts her that she will need the witch's magic wand. She will need the energy and hope of change, the magical capacity to alter things, a capacity that comes to her by virtue of the mother complex.

The magic wand and the ability to change things are crucial, for fleeing alone will accomplish nothing. The moment that the witch is close at hand, when the girl has nearly been taken in again by the attitude that the witch embodies, she changes Roland into a pond and herself into a duck. This is an image of tranquility and meditation. There is no forgetting that the threat is close at hand. But the present moment is one in which nothing can intrude as long as resistance is maintained to the lure of the appetite. The destructive part of the self offers something for the appetite. Opting for tranquility and meditation is a way of avoiding the temptation to take the bread—to seize the destructive power that offers itself.

In this version of the tale, it is Roland who is transformed into a pond, whereas in other versions it is the woman. But this is an apt image for a relationship between a man and a woman who is still under the thumb of a mother complex. The man is called on to play a sustaining, maternal role. The duck, an animal that can move equally on land and water and in air, is an expression of the many ways that the girl can elude the pursuit of the witch.

Stay with yourself, keep your center of gravity, the story recommends, if you want to escape the clutches of power and violence. Know that it can be seductive, but don't go for the bait.

PAINTING FROM THE IMAGINATION

We capture these "fleeting" images by painting them. Using this medium, it is often easier to feel their emotional impact and their meaning for our lives. During the act of painting, images may also take on a different form, which offers an opportunity to witness a psychic process as it is taking place. Guided fantasy, painting, and enactment are all ways of working with symbolic images. Each of us has to find out what method works best at a given time to help get in touch with our inner images.

One Participant's Fantasy and Image (40 years old)

After being led on a wild goose chase by those drops of blood, I am so mad at being fooled that I want to take revenge. I hurry into the tower of a castle, from where I can see the girl fleeing. Far, far away I see Roland and the stepdaughter. Nearly exploding with anger, I put on my seven-league boots. "I'll get you," I'm thinking. Then suddenly I am the girl. I am terrified of my mother and afraid that the transformation won't work. Just in the nick of time I turn into a lake and lie there completely still, as if playing dead. The lake is big enough for a duck to swim around in the middle.

The next scene is also very frightening, before and during the transformation into a flower. I can hardly do anything, I am so afraid of my mother. The other thing that makes it so difficult to take action is that I am not sure who I am, mother or stepdaugh-

ter. I am always both, and if I am only one or the other, I destroy
a part of myself. This makes me feel angry and helpless.

The woman who wrote down this fantasy said that as a child she
had often been irritated with the person she was. For her younger
sister she was a second mother, but for her mother she was a small
child. She called her brothers and sisters "the kids" until her mid-
twenties. "The thing that irritates me the most is that I don't know
what to do with my anger. It always ends up coming back at me."

In her fantasy she sees herself both as mother and daughter. She
can speak for both. The mother's anger at being fooled came very
clearly to expression, but so did the daughter's fear of the mother.
The scene from the story brought a personal mother-daughter conflict to expression. The woman concerned was different from the
heroine of the folktale in that she was not prepared to sever herself
so radically from her mother. She was not prepared to sacrifice the
power that she gained from her identification with such a powerful
mother. Neither did she care to be a mother with only a limited
share of power. This is why she transforms herself only in the last
minute.

In the picture that she painted of this scene (see figures 2 and 3),
we can see a clear identification with the ferocious mother in the
boot. The feeling she is expressing here is that her mother sees
everything she does. The fantasy and the picture about the folktale
provided a forum for thinking and feeling about the issue of separation from her mother. Her mother's rage can be compared with the
rage of all mothers who feel they have been betrayed, abandoned
when their children go their own way despite their sense of owner-
ship. The fear that she expressed in her fantasy can be compared to
the fear that all children have of their mothers, of being trampled
by them, of being exposed to their ever-observing eye. The same
thing takes place on an intrapsychic level as well: the fury that follows disappointment, its crushing weight, the feeling that in spite
of mother's physical absence she is still somehow there, watching,

preventing us from doing what we want, making us feel guilty about doing what we have to do. This is what happens when the mother complex dominates the ego complex.

The different pictures that are painted of the folktale make it clear how differently its images can be seen. Another, very different picture of the witch was painted by a fifty-six-year-old woman (see figure 1). This witch looks like a pasture. In folklore, witches often reside in pastures. As funny as this witch may look, I am not so sure I would like to get in her way. She may have disguised herself. She may have tried to make herself look harmless. Plus, what wavelength was she on?

In the painting exercise we make our own images by borrowing those of the folktale. The images that we thus create tell us a great deal about ourselves, for instance that we experience a witchlike part of ourselves when we are alone and when we are with others. Folktale-guided fantasy provides a good entry into painting as well as enactment.

PART THREE

Following the relaxation exercise, I read the tale from the transformation into a thicket to the transformation into a stone. The participants allow the images to arise from each scene. Today more time is allowed for the development of individual images. The folktale-guided fantasies, reflections on the folktale's themes, and personal reflections in relation to the themes are shared with the group.

The witch's second attack is dodged when the girl turns herself into a pretty flower in the middle of a thorny hedge, and Roland into a fiddle player. The witch knows who is hiding in the flower. As she is about to pick this flower, demonstrating the classic greed of the witch who lives by the rule of possessiveness, Roland plays a dance tune. According to this well-known motif, demonic energies cannot resist more refined and differentiated feelings. In the face of the elaborate "trouble" that such a performance entails, an unrefined energy field can only dance itself to death. The girl's escape depends on two factors. First, she makes use of nature's own "thorny" and complicated ways, making herself unreachable and unavailable. Second, the differentiated expression of feelings helps her out of the danger of self-destructive thoughts. Viewing Roland now as the masculine part of herself, she takes action.

Putting the two figures together as a couple, we would have to say that she is pretty, but not yet completely of this world. She is still guarded somewhat by a thorny hedge, still somewhat of a Sleeping Beauty whenever the mother complex comes knocking at her door. By contrast, Roland puts people in a good mood. I invited the group to play this scene to help make it more experiential.

A good deal of time was taken to play the scene. The witch, the flower, and Roland were played in turns by individuals, while the rest of the group formed a hedge. Everyone agreed that the least exciting part to play was that of the flower. One person said that it was boring being pretty, waiting, hoping not to be seen. This experience helped the interpretation along. A young woman who resembled this flower would be passive and unapproachable. Her partner would probably be more active, and he would be able to say why she is so passive: If she were to take action, she would run the risk of being taken in by the negative mother complex. She would run the risk of disparaging herself, engaging in self-destructive or even violent behavior.

The most intense experience came with the enactment of the "ordered aggression." The hedge had no problem playing out its aggression, since that was its job. It was quite interesting that several participants who thought of themselves as nonviolent played this sadistic game—on order—with gusto. The figure of the witch from the beginning of the tale was perhaps not as far from consciousness as originally assumed.[45] The witch in the story is now dead. It would seem that the destructive mother complex had

exhausted its energy, that the girl had severed her ties to this domi-
nating mother, that she could now enter freely into her relationship
with her beloved Roland. So it would seem.

So why doesn't Roland take his bride-to-be with him when he
goes to his father to announce his marriage? Something that strikes
one as odd when reading the tale becomes completely incomprehensible when it is enacted. Roland evokes rage. Experiences of
abandoning and of being abandoned come forth. Neither is the girl
spared negative comments. Why doesn't she go with him? Why
does she simply let herself be left behind? "I'll wait," she says. Her
time has not yet come. She reacts like someone who has been abandoned. She turns into a stone. She is deactivated. Only the red
color suggests that there is any hope for a turn toward new life.

What are we to make of this situation? It appears that neither
Roland nor the girl is altogether conscious of what relationships
require. Maybe Roland too grew up under the influence of a negative mother image. We could also see the witch as an image of a
destructive maternal image that affects everyone in the vicinity. This
provides the only satisfactory explanation for why Roland leaves his
love there alone. In another, more elaborate, version of the tale, he
has been warned not to let his mother kiss him, but then he forgets
the warning—and forgets his bride. He regresses back into his family of origin, or back into a previous stage of emotional growth in
which he neglects his partner. It certainly is a bad thing that he
would forget her after they have gone through so much toil and
trouble together. Or is it that he doesn't like her the way she is?

As far as the girl is concerned, the complex that has dominated
her life until now is dead and gone from the scene. But this has also
left behind a certain emptiness. Much of who she was came from
who she wasn't. "I'm not like my mother," she told herself as she
avoided the kind of power games that her mother played. So now
she has the task of finding out who she is without opposition to
someone else. She must learn this by reaching into her own depths,

including the depths of her good mothering experiences. Roland is certainly not playing the role of the good mother at the moment. And that is the way it has to be, for a man can never permanently replace a good mother. She has to bake this new self in her own kitchen.

PART FOUR

We continued in the same manner as previously, beginning with the stone and ending with the wedding. The group now divided into two sections, one of which chose to paint the scene, while the other enacted it. Their choice was based on their experiences from the first three parts, and whether painting or dramatization had provided them with more intense contact with the folktale's images.

The fantasies that emerged here dealt with the stages of the girl's transformation, which corresponded to the phases of the grieving process. In the folktale, the flower expresses a kind of suicidal apathy; she says she will probably be stepped on. In the group we experienced the change into a flower as a move toward new life and new pastures, not without its risks, as if to say, "I just want this one last taste of life, even if it's going to kill me." This passionate grasping for life and pushing oneself to the limit to find out whether it is one's fate to end in death or in life is a typical experience of persons going through grieving processes.[46] It is not the flower's fate to be stepped on; she is discovered by a shepherd, who takes her home and puts her in a cabinet where he can admire her beauty.

The transformation of a woman into a flower is a recurring motif in folktales. Often it symbolizes mourning. A woman waits in the form of a flower until her lover finds her. Perhaps this is where the expression "wallflower" comes from. Someone who turns into a flower sacrifices a great deal of freedom. Flowers have to stay put. The only thing they have to say is how beautiful they are, but this beauty is already on the wane. She is completely dependent on someone noticing her, admiring her, and turning her back into a woman while something can still be done about it. If he is too late, she wilts. We could thus take the flower to symbolize hope for change and for a new commitment to life.

The enactment strongly underlined how important it was to see the lonely flower's beauty, to admire her and dote on her. The idea of being put away in a cabinet wasn't entirely appealing, suggesting being laid in one's coffin, although symbolically the coffin can also be a vessel of transformation. In the group this image was understood as the protection that the flower needed. A woman who has not yet come completely out of her flowerhood is delicate and vulnerable; she needs to be careful. An intense relationship at this point would be too much. The flower now makes her home with a shepherd, someone who keeps and tends, and who has a close relationship with nature. She is with a man who can unite his maternal qualities with his masculinity (see figure 4).

The girl's transformation from a stone to a flower to a woman symbolizes a new birth into life through the agency of a second, positive mother. She had to go through this to be prepared to enter into a real relationship. Her first relationship with Roland was more love on the run than something that came from the depths of her being.

Many women need a relationship with a younger man into order to work their way out of a mother complex. The relationship usually lasts as long as is necessary for her to reach the level of autonomy that is appropriate for her age. Then she is ready to enter into a search for her self,[47] a self that is not defined in relation to a man. In the story, the girl turns down the invitation to marry the shepherd.

Mysterious things take place in the shepherd's home. The shepherd has no idea of who is doing the housework. Indirectly, the flower draws attention to herself, for she needs to be recognized to be transformed. An old woman offers advice: a white cloth should be thrown over the flower. The color white suggests a transition and a new beginning. Throwing the cloth over the flower indicates that the shepherd is not going to look at the woman as if she were a mere flower. He refuses her this kind of attention, covering her so that she can emerge in a new form. She is compelled to go through with this transformation.

It is time for her to take leave of her flowerhood. As a flower she was admired, but scarcely honored as an equal. She did her chores meekly, in secret, not daring to show herself. The wise woman, an aspect of the mother archetype, conveys the necessity of this move out of the "secret flower" phase of her being. But she does not want to marry the shepherd. Her relationship to him was another "transitional relationship," necessary for a time but not for good. Here the girl brings up the subject of faithfulness. She would like to be faithful to her beloved Roland. And yet she also agrees to stay with the shepherd. This stage of her growth seems to be very slow and careful.

The development from stone to woman was enacted by the group with real verve. The group was enlivened by the person who gave an excellent performance as the shepherd. Everyone wanted to be the precious flower so that they could be discovered by him. Some of the participants agreed to be the stone, given the assurance that they would get out of their petrified, depressed state. It turned out that the transition from stone to flower was not all that easy an emotional task. But it was not a hardship of desperation, as described in the folktale, so much as a hardship of reinvesting one's energy and faith in the world. Naturally, everyone felt much more exposed and vulnerable as a flower than as a stone. Some of them experienced the transition from flower to woman in a very existential way, as a rebirth into a new identity. These enactments were amply fleshed out with personal material. It was interesting to see what kind of flowers they saw themselves as.

PART FIVE

First we imagined the recognition scene, and then we looked back at all the individual scenes, and discussed what each participant had gained for him- or herself by working with the folktale.

The end of the story consisted of the so-called recognition scene. Did Roland recognize his beloved? Even more to the point, did he recognize her singing? With her singing, and with her song, she communicates something of her innermost being, recognition of which means nothing less than "knowing" (i.e., loving) him[48]—"and suddenly everything about her came back to his heart." His feelings for her came alive again. He discovered her anew. Relationship is now possible, whether on the objective level, or with the inner masculine potential of her own psyche.

There was some criticism in the group that Roland needed to do some work on himself too. The male participants especially found that the tale lacked any description of his path of development. It should be said that the shepherd can also be seen as a part of Roland. His "development" thus consisted of keeping and tending, of admiring without demanding, of supporting the girl's growth. There are of course other folktales that tell of a hero callously leaving his bride, for instance, "The King of the Golden Mountain."[49]

An Imagination on the Recognition Scene (by the same woman as above)

I am in the shepherd's home, keeping house, sad and silent. I have resigned myself to the fate of being left behind. Where could I have gone? When I hear the news of Roland's wedding, I am deeply shaken. More than ever I feel disappointed and lose my hope for a life that has more friendship and happiness than before. I can't bear to witness Roland's wedding and festivities, let alone sing for him. There is too much pain.

But I am forced to go, and so I resign myself once more. The wedding takes place in a kind of monastery. All the girls in the entire land stand in a long line in the cloister. Roland is sitting on his horse. At first I am standing at the front of the line, but when my turn comes I quickly go to the back of the line again. I am carrying my newborn baby, who is lying on my left shoulder. When I change places in the line of girls, I experience a nervous and yet exciting feeling of "Know me or know me not."

When I am the only one left and have to decide what to do, I sing, "There was a king from Thule, true to the day he died." The minute I start singing, Roland recognizes my voice, rides up to me, jumps off his horse, and embraces me. The curse has been broken. I have been redeemed. Finally I have won my freedom to love Roland and live with him.

The image of the newborn baby came from a dream the woman had had that morning. The day before, she had experienced the dramatic transformation of the flower into a woman with great intensity. In the morning she awoke with the image of the newborn baby lying on her left shoulder, and she felt very happy.

The song of the king comes from Goethe's *Faust*, as sung by Gretchen in the dungeon scene. She said, "When we were reading *Faust* in school, the teacher asked me if I could sing the song to the accompaniment of his violin. Everything came together: the thing I am going through now, the dungeon scene, and the sad song."

This song gave a melody to the girl's present emotional state, including her despair and her faithfulness. By means of it, Roland knew her. Being recognized may well be what this woman needs to get through her loneliness.

CLOSING THE GROUP WORK

We concluded by thinking and talking one more time as a group about possible interpretations for some of the folktale's scenes. This arose out of the need of some participants to look at the relation between their personal images and the universal issues that came to expression in the story.

The reports that came back about their experiences were very mixed. Several people said that it was a very gentle and yet deep method for finding out more about oneself and one's images. Emphasis was placed on the importance of discovering one's own images and the inspiration that they contained. Others were of the opinion that the story provided a way of escaping the very issues that it raised. This was in part "comforting" and in part problematic. (As a group leader, I consciously avoid blocking escape routes.) Some of the participants were convinced that they had made significant progress with issues in their lives.

Emotional experiences with folktales that take place in the group can be vital, as well as the reflections that come after them. The dilemma for the leader is whether to take the limited time that is available to plunge into the group process or to work through the text more thoroughly. My inclination is to work through the text as a whole, so that the problems, complications, and openings to new vistas, described ever again in the folktale, may become both emotionally real and intellectually satisfying.

THE WHITE SHIRT, THE HEAVY SWORD, AND THE GOLDEN RING

Folktales Integrate Dreams into a Developmental Structure

The similarity between dreams and folktale motifs need not be argued. When we amplify a dream with a folktale, we place it in a larger context of meaning suggested by a story that deals with the same issue. This process can contribute to greater emotional understanding of one's own story and themes in life.

Folktales are also very useful for making more out of dreams that do not seem to lead to any solution or point to any obvious development; the folktale offers the dream a structure-building matrix out of which it may "hatch"—a process that is quite different from simply comparing dream motifs with folktale motifs. In order for this process to work, the basic theme of the folktale has to correspond sufficiently to one of the dreamer's most important issues.

The method of using folktales in therapy is based on the idea that narrative processes in folktales can stimulate growth processes in the psyche, even in cases of resistance to the folktale, which stimulates greater consciousness of a given issue. The forward-looking thrust of folktales sparks the dimension of hope that in dreams is often present only in a latent and potential form.

Case Example

A thirty-five-year-old teacher has the feeling he has not yet discovered his true calling. He is thinking of becoming a playwright or a filmmaker. He embarks on several creative projects, but, frustrated when he cannot achieve his goals more rapidly, he abandons his most promising projects. He cannot understand why he gets in his own way. He comes to therapy with the hope of finding out what he should do with his life. He feels disoriented and indecisive, and wants to change that. His indecisiveness is especially problematic in his relationships. He has had many experiences with women with whom he feels he has repeatedly played the role of the rescuer. He raised them "out of the gutter," helped them get off drugs, find work, and so on. Once they are in better shape, they leave him—at least this is how he sees it. In the course of therapy, it turns out that once the women he has been seeing are doing well again, he loses interest in them.

In his family, he was the youngest child, the only boy of three children. His mother and sisters experienced him as someone who spoils others. Although his father had been emotionally and physically present to only a limited degree, he exploded from time to time when it came to issues of child rearing, at which times he behaved unfairly, which provoked his mother to compensate with generosity and spoiling.

Peter, as I will call him, had a sense of being talented as a child, even though he was a bit of a dreamer. He could paint and write poems, but he could also play soccer and was a good actor. School was no problem for him, although he did not realize the height of his abilities since he always involved himself in so many activities. If he got into a tight spot, he was inevitably rescued by some "lucky coincidence." Since the age of eighteen, he had repeatedly dreamed the following dream: *I am on a ship in the middle of the sea. The ship is stable and well equipped, but I have lost my orientation. I am nervous but not too nervous, since the ship is solid. Someone will sail over this way at some point.*

The ship varies from dream to dream. Sometimes he is alone on the ship, sometimes with others. The feeling of disorientation and wishing for help are constants. These dreams leave him with a long-lasting feeling of disorientation, but also with the slight consolation that things are not really that bad. It is noteworthy that the dreamer is always sure that help will come his way. This certainly seems to prevent him from doing anything to save himself. Although the end of many dreams gives us a clue as to how to proceed, this dream ends simply with waiting. To me this did not give the impression of an especially productive, but rather of an apathetic sort of waiting.

Two dreams came after a year of therapy; they were what gave me the incentive to introduce a folktale into therapy. *A gray old man is threatening me. "This is a joke," I think to myself. "I'm much stronger than him." But that old man is just as tough as any young man. I'm not sure how I'm going to fight him off. I wake up feeling bad.*

Convinced that the old man was much stronger, Peter suffered terribly from his feeling of defenselessness. In association to the old man, Peter thought of old men and dwarfs in folktales who look so harmless and then turn out to be incredibly strong. He was afraid that the old man in his dream was a really evil figure, someone with a dangerous mixture of life experience and resignation, which could only result in evil intentions. Peter was quite able to see this "grayness" as a part of his own personality. He was well aware of how this inner old man "attacked" him: whenever he felt there was no use in doing anything, he would tear everything down with his negativity. He felt he had no defense against this part of himself, as in the dream. A month later he had another dream: *I am shut in a cage. I can feel the metal bars, but I can't see anything. I must be blind. Together with me in the cage are cats and other soft, furry animals. I hold them close to comfort myself. I feel miserable.*

Peter's associations: I couldn't stand being blind. It made me feel just awful. It was the same feeling I had on those ships in my dreams on the high seas when I felt so disoriented. The cats made me feel better. That reminds me of how it is when I sleep with a woman just for warmth and comfort and she doesn't make any big deal out of it and just enjoys it as well.

I feel so caged in. I've put myself behind bars. But blind? Am I blind to what I am doing with myself?

The dreamer is well able to link his dreams with what he experiences on an everyday basis. And yet there is something in his dreams that cannot be explained by reference to his everyday experience. The dreams are lacking in dynamic. There is no forward pulse, other than the suggestion that he should wake up. The second dream also prodded him to wake up, to open his eyes and take a look around. Dreams that do not go anywhere may well suggest that it might help to look at what is going on without running away. Peter is the sort of person who always waits until "someone comes along." He has no problem hanging around until that happens. Taking a look at what is going on is not quite as easy.

I decided I would let him take a folktale home with him. I had just read it, and I was impressed with its similarity to his dreams.

THE STORY[50]

A king took a wife who was noble in lineage but lowly in spirit. She violated his trust every day. A year later she bore him a son who was white and red just like milk and bread. His beauty increased every day. The more he grew, the more he fulfilled his father's expectations. He grew up to be one of the most intelligent, noble, and hard-working boys in the entire kingdom. Everyone who knew him said he was handsome and good. When he turned eighteen and was in his prime, the queen fell into illicit love with him. She decided secretly that she would make him her spouse at any cost. She knew this could never come about in her own castle, and she was afraid that if she said anything to him, he would tell his father. So she made plans to seduce him in a distant land. There it would be easier to satisfy her desire.

Soon it was the handsome prince's birthday. The king gave a huge party for him. In the morning, musicians from all the regiments of the army would accompany services in the church. At two o'clock in the afternoon, there would be a great feast to which several thousand guests would be invited. In the evening, everything would be set to glow in blazing torchlight: the castle, its gardens, each and every house in the city. There would be fireworks everywhere one went.

Everything went off as planned. When worship was over, the queen took her son into the garden and filled his head with such sweet talk that he didn't even notice that they were leaving the castle grounds. When they came to the edge of a body of water so large you couldn't see the other side, he still didn't realize what was going on. A marvelous ship awaited them. "What a beautiful house that is sitting there on the water," the prince exclaimed—he had never seen a ship before. "From here you can only see how it looks from the outside," said the queen. "The inside is even grander than the castle." "That I would like to see," said the young man. She took him aboard and sat down with him in room after room. After occupying themselves in this manner for a few hours, the prince said, "Mother dear, soon the feast will begin. We'd better hurry back home so we'll be there in time. We wouldn't want to make my father and all the guests wait." "There's no hurry," answered the queen. But he was in a hurry, and went out onto the deck. What a surprise when, instead of grass, he saw only sky and water in every direction. The queen had made a deal with the captain that he would stop at the appointed time at the castle gardens, pull up the anchor as soon as they were on board, and set sail for a foreign country. The prince was so upset he could hardly contain himself. "Mother, this swimming house is a house of thieves. We have been kidnapped!" "Calm down, Son," said the queen. "I only wanted to play a practical joke on you. We will be docking again soon." That was no lie, and soon the prince saw a dark spot in the distance that grew bigger and bigger the closer they got. Soon it was a mighty forest of oaks. The ship came to rest at harbor, and the queen took her son by the hand. "Let's get out now. You'll be happy soon."

Going ashore, they entered a pleasant forest. The prince kept asking if this was another one of the king's pleasure gardens, and if they would be home again soon. But the queen skillfully avoided answering his questions until they came to a clearing. "Dear Son, I am tired. Let us lie down here a while and rest." When they were lying together in the grass, she kissed him and told him she loved him. She admitted that she had abducted him, and told him he had to become her husband or else she would die. The prince pulled away brusquely. "Dear Mother, I hope you see what a terrible mistake it would be if we did that. It can't happen now, and it will never happen." He didn't budge an inch, whatever the queen said. When she saw that there was no chance, she began to hate him, and her hatred grew more intense than her love had ever been. But she kept it hidden from him, and went on speaking to him in a friendly tone, pretending that her proposal had only been a way to test his virtue.

After resting for a while, they went on deeper into the forest until evening time. Suddenly they came into view of a castle high up in the distance. "Dear Mother," said the prince, "stay here while I go over to that castle and find out who's living there. If it's not a castle of crooks, I'll come back and get you." She agreed, and he went. The gates were open, so he went into the courtyard and on into the castle, where he discovered everyone cast into a deep sleep: servants, chambermaids, cooks, stablehand, and cowhand. After wandering through the entire castle, he finally came to a splendid hall with high ceilings and a round golden table in the middle. Sitting on the table were a white shirt and a golden ring. Around the edge of the table was written in silver, "Whoever puts this shirt on will command the sword on the wall. Whoever takes this ring in his mouth will understand the language of the birds." Looking up, he saw a mighty broadsword hanging on the wall. Being skilled at the art of fencing, he tried to take it in his hands and swing it through the air a few times, but he wasn't able to lift it off the nails it was sitting on. The white shirt and the ring he was able to put on, and as soon as he had done so, he immediately felt like a different person—it was as if fresh new blood were flowing in his veins. He leaped back to the wall, removed the sword, and flashed it through the air like a mere toy.

Just then he heard the sound of footsteps echoing from the castle halls, as if a hundred people were running about. The door flew open and three servants in shining suits entered. "What is the desire of our king and lord?" they asked. At first he was surprised, but quickly replied, "I need an elegant coach to go and pick up my mother who is waiting at the edge of the forest." The servants bowed and went about their task. After they left, the prince continued his inspection of the hall. In the corner, behind a curtain, he found an old man with gray hair sleeping in a bed. His face looked false, like the face of a man from whom nothing good could be expected. The prince tried to wake him up, but the old man just turned over, kept on snoring into his white beard, and went back to sleep. Just then the prince's mother arrived in the coach. Pleased at the sight of the beautiful castle, she planned to make it her home. But the coals of revenge were still glowing in her heart. Day and night she brooded on how to ruin the good prince. Friendlier than ever, she told him every day how happy she was to have such a son and how she loved him more than anything in the whole world.

After spending a few days in the castle, the prince went out one day for a walk in the woods. There he heard a pitiful moaning and groaning that sounded as if it were coming from out of the ground. He swished his sword to summon his servants and asked them where the sound was coming from and who was doing the groaning. "We don't know," the servants told him. "The only one who knows is the old man who is sleeping in the hall. He has all the keys to the underground chambers." The prince ordered them to fetch the old man. He refused to come until the prince threatened to bring him by force if need be. That made him come, and he brought his key ring with him. When he pulled out a stone in the wall, a little door opened into a dark corridor. "Go in there," he grumbled to the prince. The prince was smart enough to make the old man go in first. The farther they went into the corridor, the closer they seemed to get to the moaning. Finally they came to a second iron door, and when the old man opened it, they saw there a dark hole into which all of the waste waters of the castle were flowing. In the middle of this putrid hole a girl was sitting wearing rotting clothes. When she saw the old man she said, "Leave me alone, or give me death to end my misery." The prince stepped forward and ordered the old man to take the girl out of the hole. He hesitated, but when the prince raised his sword, he did as he was ordered. The young woman begged for mercy. "Please don't take me out into the daylight until I have something to wear. I would rather die." The prince calmed her with a friendly voice. "You have been rescued

*from your hell. You shall have whatever you desire." Then he put
the old man back into the castle and sent two servants to the young
woman to wash her, dress her in fine garments, and feed her with
solid food, so that she could begin to recover. After a while, she
came out of her dark chamber. She was beautiful. Her hair was so
golden it looked as if the sun itself had ornamented her head with
its rays of light. Her eyes were as blue as the sky at dusk. Her face
was as fine as if it had been painted with roses and lilies. The
prince's heart leaped for joy when he saw her. Unable to restrain
himself, he went straight to her and offered her his hand in a ges-
ture of friendly greeting. He took her inside the castle, and asked
her where she had come from and how she had landed in such a
revolting prison. "I am a princess," she replied. "My father's kingdom is on the other side of the lake. One day I was walking with
my servants along the shore of the lake. Pirates landed their ship,
stole everything I had, and took me with them. They sold me to the
bad old man who used to rule this house. He pestered me day and
night, trying to get me to be his wife. When I told him I never
wanted to see him again, he threw me in that stinking hole. Every
three days he brought me bread and water and asked me if I was
ready to change my mind. But I never did, and I have been there
ever since, turning into the thing that you found."*

*Now pity and love make good partners, and as soon as the
prince heard this story, love was running thick in his veins. "You
refused the old man's hand," he said. "And now I offer you mine. I
cannot live without you. If you choose not to be my wife, still I will
have no other." The beautiful princess liked the prince better than
the old man, so she said, in all innocence, "I like you so much that I
can't imagine marrying anyone else." They kissed and danced
about together. In this merry mood they came to the old queen.
When she heard this it was as if a knife had pierced her heart. Now
she hated the prince twice and three times as much. She said in a
cynical tone, "I am happy that you have found such a beautiful and
worthy young woman, my son, and that I have found such a lovely
daughter-in-law. The greatest fortune in all the world couldn't
make me feel happier than I feel right now. Prepare yourselves for*

the wedding, my dear children; I'll take care of everything else. I hope you are as happy as I!" She embraced the prince and the beautiful young woman. Secretly she was thinking, "Just you wait, you'll be soaking wet soon." "But we can't celebrate the wedding here," said the young woman. "We have to do it at my parents' house. I really need to visit them; they are so worried about me. Let me go now, and let my future husband come along after me." "Now I have an even greater admiration of you," replied the queen. "Now I see what a truly loving daughter you are. Go ahead; in a year and a day I will come with my dear son and we will celebrate the wedding in high style." But she thought to herself, "As soon as you are gone, my dear girl, I'll do away with him." The prince had a ship prepared, and within three days the princess set sail. The old queen had pressured the captain of the ship into forcing the princess to marry him no matter how he did it.

Once the ship was at sea, the captain approached her, hoping to win her over. But she didn't show the slightest inclination. So he told her, "Here is your choice: either make me your man and tell your father the king that I saved you—or else get ready to sink to the bottom of this lake. You have three days to think it over." Once she was alone again, she sank to her knees and begged God to rescue her from this nightmare. And she was blessed with a good idea. When the captain came back on the third day to hear her answer, she told him, "A year and a day, then we shall wed." The captain was satisfied with this answer. When they reached land again, he took her to visit her parents, and told them a story about how he had rescued her from a stinking cave and how he aspired to marry her. The king and queen were so happy to see their child again that they agreed right away for the wedding to be held in a year and a day. Then the young woman spoke. "When I was lying in that cave I made a vow—a vow I must keep. I vowed that if I ever got out, I would serve at an inn that would be open to everyone. I would offer free food and lodging to any pilgrim or wanderer who came along." The king didn't like this idea at all. He wasn't about to hear of his princess of royal lineage going to work in the slums. But the queen countered, "If you make a promise to God, you have to keep it; if you don't, you'll be punished as sure as the sun shines in the sky. Get your inn going. Do the work that you promised. It won't harm you a bit." So an inn was built that was visited by many travelers and pilgrims, all of whom found sustenance there. They blessed the pious princess and prayed to God for her to be rewarded. Let us leave the princess with her work for now, and return to the prince.

When the princess was gone and the bad queen still couldn't find a way to seduce the prince, she at last turned to the old man for help. He agreed to help her on the condition that she promised to be his wife. She happily agreed. "Have him visit the lion's den in the castle moat," he instructed. "The beasts will tear him limb from limb." The queen lay on her bed and pretended that she was dying. The prince became distressed and asked her again and again what he might possibly do to help. "There is something that can be done, but it is fraught with danger. You could easily come to harm, and I would rather die than have anything happen to you." "I'm not afraid of anything, dear Mother," said the prince. "After all, it is a matter of life and death." "You are such a good son. Well then," she conceded, "I'll tell you. If I can hold a lion's cub on my breast, its strength will soak in through my skin and within a day I will be well again." The prince went straight to the lion pit, entered without the least trepidation, and since lions don't harm those of noble blood, they let him go in peace. When he took one of the cubs, the lioness got up and roared at him. But the prince gave her such a fearsome look that she sat back down again. The queen put the young cub on her breast and said, "I feel better now, my strength has returned, I have been healed." But the lion cub didn't stay still, and stuck out its claws. "That's enough," she screamed. "Take him away and kill him. I don't ever want to see him again." The prince took the lion and said, "Why should I kill the poor little animal that saved my dear mother's life? I'll take him back to his mother where I got him." He took the lion cub back to the pit. The old lioness roared for joy at having her cub back again.

The queen's plan was foiled, and so she returned to the old man to work out a plan about how to get even with the prince. "There is only one thing to do. You have to get him to take off his shirt. Once he's lost his strength, he won't be able to swing the sword anymore. Then we'll be able to put him in his place." The queen invited a large group of guests, and went to the prince. "To thank you for saving my life," she told him, "I have ordered a great feast in your honor. Come and sit down next to me so that we can celebrate together." The prince was very pleased and followed her into the hall in which the guests had already gathered. By the end of the feast, he had gotten quite involved in conversation with his friends. She took the opportunity to pour a sleeping potion into his cup. "Long live my son, who saved my life," she proposed as she raised her glass. He drank the contents of the cup in one swig. Soon the guests were on their way home and the prince felt so tired he went right to bed and fell asleep. The queen and the old man sneaked into his room and removed his white shirt. The old man then put it on, and gave a knife to the queen. "Take this and put out his left eye." After she did this, the man dug out the other eye and threw the prince into the lion's pit.

The pain roused the prince immediately from his slumber. Now his mother's cruelty was no longer a secret to him, nor had he failed to hear the old man gloating over his deed. When he realized that he was being thrown into the lion pit, he was glad because he assumed that the lion would swallow him right up. He didn't mind, for he felt he had lived long enough. But things didn't turn out quite the way he anticipated. Instead, the lioness came to him and whimpered sadly. The lion cub came and licked his wounds until they were healed again. Every day the lioness brought him a piece of meat and put it on his knee. He ate it raw; it was his only source of nourishment. The lions brought the meat to him through an underground passageway that went from the lion pit into the forest. One day the prince felt around in the pit, discovered the passageway, and climbed inside. At first the air was thick and heavy, but after a while, he could breathe more easily, and gradually he noticed that the tunnel was growing larger and that fresh air was blowing his way.

Soon he heard birds singing in the trees. Deer were running

about. He felt the warm sun on his face. He prayed and thanked God for his escape. On he went, as well as he could. Toward evening he heard a sound in the distance. Walking toward the sound, he came to the ocean. A ship had just landed to take on more fresh water. The captain of the ship saw the young lad and took pity on him, he looked so forlorn wandering about. So he asked him if he would like to come aboard. "Yes, please. Otherwise I would die of hunger," said the prince. The captain did his best to take care of him, and his spirits improved a little each day. When the ship came to land again, he gave the captain many thanks before disembarking and going back into the streets.

One day he came to a big city. A woman standing in front of the gates called to him, "Come to my house. All poor travelers and pilgrims will be taken care of." He put out his hand and she led him into the house, where he was provided with a good meal and a very comfortable bed. Before he fell asleep, the woman came and sat down next to him. "Tell me your story. That is my payment." "I would rather forget it," answered the prince. "It is such a sad tale. But if you insist, I will tell it." So he told her everything that had happened. Her interest mounted as he told how he had saved a beautiful young woman from out of a hole and how they had promised to marry. Suddenly she embraced him and told him amid passionate sobs, "You are the one. Imagine finding you again like this!" He was overjoyed to meet her again. But his joy left him again as soon as he told her about what his mother and that wicked old man had done to him. Neither could she control her tears when she looked at him and his empty eye sockets.

When he had finished telling his story, she found him some fine clothing and took him to her father. "Dear Father, today is the happiest day of my life. The good Lord has given me back my true rescuer and only true husband." She bade him tell the king the whole story again. The king believed what he heard, but once the initial excitement at seeing her long lost lover had subsided, he became irritated at the prospect of her marriage to a blind man. Even so, he found it the lesser of evils for her to marry the boy—who at least was a prince—rather than the captain of a ship. So he made it clear that the captain had better disappear. And in a hidden part of the royal gardens, a small castle was built where a secret wedding was held for the prince and princess. They moved into the castle, where they received nothing to eat except what had been cooked in the king's kitchen. They had to make their own clothes from cloth spun and woven by the princess both day and night.

The local squires were not happy about this marriage, for they had been deprived of the feasting, ball, and entertainment that they had grown accustomed to. Neither were they pleased at the prospect of being ruled by a blind king one day. So they plotted to tumble down the walls of the little castle inhabited by the prince and princess as soon as they could.

One evening the prince and princess went out of their little castle into their little garden to enjoy the fresh, cool air, and sat down under a tall lime tree. The prince removed the golden ring from his finger. The ring was the only thing that he had been able to take with him from his former home. With the thought of amusing himself by listening to what the birds were saying, he put the ring into his mouth. Just then three crows flew into the lime tree and began talking to each other. "I know something you don't know," said the first crow. "What?" asked the other two. "We know something too." "Over at the mayor's place a horse fell down. There's going to be a fine meal. How delicious it will be!" The second crow said, "I know something else that if those two over there knew, they wouldn't just be sitting there." "What?" asked the other two. "Tonight at ten o'clock that little castle will be blown to bits by the squires." The third crow commented, "I know something that the blind prince would be glad to know." "What?" asked the other two. "Tonight between eleven and twelve o'clock a dew will fall from the sky that restores the eyesight of anyone who wipes it on their eyes. Now let's get to work on that horse before anyone else finds it." And they flew out of the tree.

Putting his ring back on his finger, the prince said to his wife, "Let's go a little farther into the forest. The evening is still pleasant." He led the way. They hadn't been gone for even half an hour when there was a sudden flash and a boom as thunderous as a

*thousand cannons all at once. The princess was so startled she
nearly collapsed. But when the prince told her the whole story, she
was relieved and thanked God for her life. They lay down under a
tree to rest. The princess soon fell asleep, but the prince stayed
awake. About twelve o'clock he felt around in the grass, gathered
up dew with his hand, and wiped it in his eye sockets. The more he
wiped, the brighter everything got. After the third time, he could
see the moon's beams shining through the trees again. Then he saw
his dear wife again, lying there so wonderfully in the moonshine.
Full of delight, he kissed her. She awoke and gazed back at her husband. She hardly knew him with eyes so clear. He filled his water
bottle with more dew and hung it around his waist so he would
have some if he ever needed it again. Thus, a greater portion of
good luck grew out of the bad luck that had befallen him. In their
poverty they were richer than rich. But they would still have to
endure even greater ordeals. Their trials were not yet over.*

*In the morning they continued on into the forest, feeding on
roots and herbs. Not used to walking, the princess soon grew tired
and at midday sat down under an oak tree, put her head in the
prince's lap, and fell asleep. Gazing at her admiringly, enjoying her
shining beauty, he noticed a little bag hanging on a string around
her neck. When he opened it, he found a ruby he liked so much
that he untied the string and examined it with care. Wondering
what it would look like if he played with it in the sunlight, he put it
down next to him in the grass. Just then the princess moved her
head off his lap and onto the pillow of leaves and moss that he had
made for her.*

*When he reached for the stone again, he saw that a raven had
taken it and was playing with it. He jumped to try to catch the
bird, but it flew off and settled in a tree out of reach. The prince
chased it and threw stones at it. The raven jumped from branch to
branch, from tree to tree, until finally it disappeared into the
bushes. Distressed, the prince gave up and decided to try to find his
way back to the place under the tree. But he couldn't find it, lost his
way, and went deeper into the forest, his spirits sinking with every
step. He met a distinguished gentleman coming from the other*

direction. The prince asked him how he might find his way back to the tree where he had left his dear sleeping wife. The man couldn't help him. "There are a thousand of those trees in this forest. You'll never find the one you're looking for. You'd be better off if you came with me." So he followed the gentleman to a beautiful white house in the middle of the forest. Inside, eleven boys were sitting enjoying themselves at a table piled high with food. The man said, "Now everyone is here. Finally all twelve are present. Stay for a year and a day and you can have all you require. But at the end of the year, you'll hear three riddles. Those who solve them will receive a bottomless sack of gold. But those who fail will lose their lives." The eleven boys let out a cheer, wished the gentleman a long life, and celebrated for an entire year. They often invited the prince to come and join in the festivities, but he was quiet and withdrawn, ate and drank very little, spoke even less, spent all of his time thinking about his poor wife. So let us see what happened to her.

When she awoke to find her husband gone, she called him for a long time, of course without any luck. Then suddenly she felt that the bag around her neck was missing. Could he have stolen my gem and run away with it? she thought, and what else could she think? The thought made her sick, and if she had not been a woman of faith, she would have taken her own life. Instead, she resigned herself to the fate that heaven intended, and went down the difficult path through the forest until she came to the ocean, where a ship was anchored. She embarked, pulled up the anchor, prayed for mercy, and sailed off for several weeks until she came to the shores of a foreign land. After walking and walking, she saw a castle in the distance—the same one from which the prince had saved her. The sight of it revived her spirits, for she hoped that she would see her husband there—if he saw her, he would certainly not turn her away. Entering the castle, she asked if the prince was there. The servants were about to tell her the story of his sad fate when the queen came in and recognized the princess. "What are you doing here?" she demanded. The princess told her she had been looking for her husband ever since she was separated from him in the forest. "Come in here with me," said the queen. The princess followed her into a room. The queen closed the doors and called the old man. She held the princess, gouged out her eyes, and threw her to the lions. "Now go and look for your husband," she said, laughing out loud. But the lions didn't eat her. The cubs licked her eyes until they were healed, and the lions brought her food to keep her alive.

Meanwhile, the year in the forest had nearly passed. The eleven boys had been too busy enjoying themselves to think about the solution to the riddles—but not the prince, who spent a lot of time pondering. One evening, when he was sitting in the forest beneath a tree, three vultures flew into it and landed in its branches. Curious about what they might say, the prince placed the ring under his tongue and listened. "Hey, Brothers," called out the first. "Tomorrow there's going to be a big party—eleven fat worker boys and one lean prince." "What do you mean?" asked the second. "Tomorrow they are supposed to have the answer to three riddles, but they haven't got a clue," said the third. "Do you know any of the answers?" asked the second. "Yes, yes, I want to say it," said the first. "No, I want to say it," said the third. "You start," said the second. The first one began, "The first riddle is, 'What is the house made of?' The second riddle is, 'Where did the food come from?' and the third, 'Why is it never night?'" "Now you tell me the answer," said the second. The third blurted out all the answers: "The house is made of the bones of hanged men, the food came from the king's table, and the daylight that never ends comes from the ruby hanging from the ceiling that the wizard stole from the prince in the forest." After finishing their chatter, they took wing. The prince was happy and slept better than he had for a whole year.

The next morning the eleven boys feasted and partied as usual. The gentleman came walking through the forest and called out from a distance, "Boys, stand at attention. It's time to answer the riddles." They lined up obediently, the prince at the end of the line. "What is the house built of?" he asked. "Bricks," said the first. "Stones," said the second. "Wood and glue," said the third. And so on until it was the prince's turn. "Of hanged men's bones," he answered. "You solved the riddle," said the gentleman. "Now tell me where the food came from." "From the kitchen," said all eleven, except the prince, who answered, "From the king's table." "You solved the riddle," said the gentleman. "Now tell me the answer to the third. Why was your house as bright at night as during the day?" "Because of the lamp," cried out all eleven at the same time. But the prince replied, "Because of the ruby that you stole from me when you turned yourself into a raven. You hung it from the ceiling."

"You guessed the answer, and here is your bottomless sack of gold," said the gentleman. While he was removing the heads of the other eleven, the prince went inside, took the ruby down from the ceiling, and set off into the forest again until he came to an ocean. He kept on going along the shoreline until he came to the nearest harbor town, where he hired a ship and sailed to the castle where his mother was. With all of the bad luck I have had, he thought, who knows whether or not I will be able to get the castle back— and my wife too.

Late that night a ship put in anchor near the castle. Disguising himself as a sailor, he went ashore and made his way to the castle, where he entered quietly. While everyone was fast asleep, he climbed onto the roof and down a chimney into a room where he found the old man sleeping. The first thing he noticed was the white shirt lying on the round golden table. He put it on, took the sword that was hanging on the wall, and inspected the entire room. The old man was lying in the same bed as before, and next to him the queen. The prince swung his sword three times. The servants came running in and greeted him as their king and lord. "Tie them together and throw them in a cage—the kind made for cows." And so it was. The queen tried to charm the prince again with lies and deceit, but it was to no avail. They tied her up and threw her into the cage.

The first thing the servants told him was that the princess had been there and had asked if they knew where he was. New hope was born in his heart. He sent someone to ask the queen where the princess was. She wouldn't say anything, nor could they find her in *the old stinking hole. Suddenly he had a bright idea. He would go to the good lion to offer his thanks—along with a really fine meal. Oxen and cows were slaughtered, and the servants brought the meat in large feeding troughs to the lion pit. He took the meat and fed the lions himself. Just imagine when he opened the door and saw his dear wife, blind, in the lion pit. He ran to her and embraced her. Once again, there was a mixture of so much sadness and so much happiness. He took her right away into the castle, where he washed her eyes with the dew from his flask. How she smiled at him! Now they had everything they wanted. They invited guests to stay for several days to celebrate their reunion. Then he wrote a letter to his father explaining everything that had happened, and traveled with his dear wife to make a personal visit. Later he sent for the cage with the queen and the old man, which he turned over to his father to carry out the punishment. They were burned publicly. The prince succeeded his father, and later he inherited his wife's kingdom. Since yet another kingdom belonged to that castle, he ended up as lord of three kingdoms.*

The initial reason for introducing this intervention was the excitement I felt when I found this folktale and saw its astonishing resemblance to the motif of my analysand's dream.

All three dreams that I have mentioned contain motifs that also occur in the folktale:

- feeling disorientation at sea
- being at the mercy of an old man
- being locked up with feline animals

The folktale's protagonist has several features that are similar to Peter's main issues:

- he is an admirable young man
- he has a close relationship with his mother, who admires him
- he has a habit of "raising women out of the gutter"

My intervention also arose out of a need I felt to increase motivation in therapy. Folktales can help here, provided they appeal to the analysand. Getting interested in the folktale could help motivate

Peter to take more responsibility for himself, and depend less on solutions coming from "someone else."

One danger of introducing a folktale into therapy is that the analysand will be frightened away from the perils of the protagonist's journey. If the analysand reaches this jumping-off place, the folktale and everything that has been accomplished with it so far will for now be discarded. Later on, it may or may not be reclaimed. In view of the fact that we therapists invest such a move with a significant amount of hope, we must also prepare ourselves for feeling disappointed if the analysand does not take us up on our invitation.

Peter's reaction was that he thought I had been extremely helpful in searching out his folktale. It unsettled him at the same time as it moved him.

THE TEMPTATION

Peter was struck with the similarity between his situation at home and that described at the beginning of the tale. Even if his mother had never explicitly expressed any sexual interest in him, the attention that she paid him was clearly more for her benefit than his, and she was not at all enthusiastic about his leading his own independent life. This was one reason he preferred to "dwell in the land of imagination," which gave him a great deal of satisfaction, even if he was not always quite sure about how to put it to use in his outer life. This uncertainty is typical of people with a positive mother complex. They feel at home in the realm of fantasy, where just about anything can happen, and they don't feel any great need to confront evil in the world. This immersion in fantasy is more likely to lead to an entrapment in the unconscious if the father is missing from the scene. The father may offer another pole for orientation.

Thus incest need not always be viewed as primarily a sexual matter; it can also represent an overextended stay—an arrest—in the realm of the mother complex. Moreover, the sexual dimension of incest also has a symbolic meaning.

In the folktale, the decisive turn of events takes place when the boy rejects his mother's advances. This is his first decisive "no," a turning away and separating from his mother. Once he says "no," a castle comes into view that symbolizes the wealth that is potentially his—that is, his future goals come into view.

Peter was under the impression that he had already positioned himself in life—that he had already staked out his territory by declining the incestuous wish. After all, he had moved away from home, and had gathered a certain amount of romantic experience. But then he was aware that he was still romantically involved with the realm of his inner fantasy, an involvement that was quite independent of his outer life. This was part of what disoriented him. He really wanted to do something in his life, but his ambitions remained largely unrealized. He admitted that he felt disturbed whenever his mother was a factor that disrupted his creative process. For instance, she would be shocked if she saw that a play he was writing had a certain sadistic twist. He never finished writing those plays.

The prince's rejection of his mother's advances was much more decisive than Peter's exclusion of his mother's disturbing influences—a conclusion he was not especially happy to reach. But then such an important "no" is not something that can simply be declared once and for all; it needs to be said over and over, in a hundred different ways.

THE VISION

Once the folktale protagonist has staked out his ground, the next thing he has to do is engage in the fight in the castle. There he finds a mysterious round table. The table's form is complete and of great value, something that is central. Peter commented that he was aware of the importance of such a golden stability in his life, but he never really believed he could achieve it. His vision of the future was still too shaky.

This part of the folktale portrays the prince's initiation into his own personal life. The shirt symbolizes his greater self, which would give him the energy he needs to realize his goals. The sword suggests his ability to be decisive and defend his rights. The ring portrays sensitivity to correspondences between things that can be seen with the naked eye and those that can be seen only with a spiritual eye. The round table points to a vision of wholeness— something that can only be achieved through a number of trials and adventures.

At this point in the story, he is granted the power of the vision. As if he could just jump into someone else's body, he is given a gift of youth and strength. The vision awakens new virtues associated with the conviction that he will have to go the way of a hero, a way that is all his own, his feet planted firmly on the ground, one ear open to the voice of the spirit. Most people have had visions, though they are not always as classic as this. A vision affords a kind of "knowledge" of the direction that one's life will be taking. We are grasped by what life has in store for us. Visions convey strength and the certainty of being able to do something with one's life. But then we may not see our visions through. We may begin taking measures in order to realize a certain vision, after which we start to wonder if the vision is really so important. Maybe we simply become distracted by other things and discard the vision as a dream of our youth.

Peter asked himself if he really had a vision. Whether or not it was really his own, the vision from the folktale did give him the sense of what it would be like to have one; he made good use of it for his own purposes. Wearing the shirt meant that he was not putting on anyone else's clothes; he was carrying his own load, and not borrowing time at someone else's expense. This strengthened his position. As to swords, he wasn't particularly fond of such military instruments, but he did want to be able to act decisively, as long as he could do so without being brutal or callous. The "power of the word"—including the potential violence of language—was something he cherished. "Having a ring" meant the ability to trust his intuition, to commit himself to a world view in which mundane things and those of the spirit are intimately connected. Until now, spiritual matters had outweighed earthly matters by far.

I asked him to tell me more about what fascinated him so much about this part of the story. It is worthwhile to gather more information about visions in order to determine if they are authentic or only assumed. Real visions give strength, whereas illusions—which require significant expenditures of energy to keep alive—only rob us of strength. There is no way to predict which visions of a folktale will speak to a particular reader. Naturally, it is a nice thing when we encounter a vision in a narrative that inspires us and makes us feel significant. Therapeutically, such experiences can be judged as authentic when they result in heightened self-esteem. Artificial illusions are not likely to have this effect. If a vision affords the right image at the right time—if it gives expression to a pressing psychic reality—it can trigger fascination and stimulate an "archetypally encapsulated hope,"[51] even if its origin is more text than psyche.

Seeking to capture the vision through photography, Peter became more motivated, hopeful, and decisive. To a certain extent, the vision became his own.

AN INITIAL CONFRONTATION WITH THE MOTHER

The young man in the story became more independent through his vision of initiation. The surge of energy is expressed in the waking up of everyone in the castle. The servants waking up and resuming their work reminds us of Sleeping Beauty. Things that have been slumbering in the prince's unconscious have become reactivated.

The first thing that the prince must do is send for his mother—nothing would have been resolved by simply leaving her behind.

Such problems can never be overcome in a single stroke; they need to be looked at again and again. Emotional growth takes time.

The problem is that her passionate love has turned into passionate hatred—all in secret. Such emotional reversals are typical among people who tend to see things in black and white, who have great difficulty accepting the ambivalence of life and who avoid the realization that most things have both a light and a dark side. The hero of our tale may well be under the influence of such a mother complex. He too could react to disappointment by twisting his unrequited love into a renunciation that cries out for revenge or death.

If we see the woman as the model of what happens when a woman is rejected by her son, then her switch to hatred shows how possessive she has been; if she cannot have her son, he should die. There is no room here for grief, and she avoids facing up to any feelings of guilt. Grief and guilt may have been emotions that would have kept her love from turning into poison.

The mother's sense of disappointment is understandable, in spite of the fact that the narrative does not leave us feeling very sympathetic with her. The young prince's intense righteousness about the violation of the incest taboo suggests strongly that the desire must be intense. Women who want to hold on to their sons are often attempting to compensate for the loss of a partner. And a son who competes with his father, trying to be a better husband, helps his mother in this attempt. The attempt to hold on to the son could thus represent an attempt to repair through her relationship with the son something that didn't go well with the husband, in the hope that relations between the sexes might turn out well after all. Once the son tears himself away from the mother, she will have to give up the illusion that the problem can be solved in this way. And then she will experience not only the anger that rightly belongs to every process of separation, but also anger at herself for having fallen into a trap. Fortunately, a mother who submits to a violent, murderous hatred is not all that common.

Peter's mother was less filled with hatred than with sadness and resignation over not being able to share anything more with him. Peter had come to the realization that it was not so much his mother's expectations that had prevented him from doing what he wanted to do. He was slowed down by his ties to something that he had difficulty describing—something nearly formless, like an ocean, pleasant and without many obstacles, although not without its dangers. And then there was his desire to have everything that could be had, and to avoid all loss. It wasn't that Peter's mother wanted to destroy him; it was just that she didn't want to let him go—and that he didn't want to fight for his freedom. As a consequence, everything associated with his mother was destructive because it deprived him of orientation, making him passive and demanding.

There is a difference between the mother figure in the folktale and in Peter's life. When a folktale figure exaggerates certain qualities, this can help to put one's own parental images into perspective, and can lead to a more precise description that avoids the kinds of extravagance that are typical in folktales. Work with folktales is not a matter of reducing myth and life to a common denominator. The story should stimulate us into reflecting on and probing into our lives. Looking at ourselves in the mirror of folktales should help us clarify how we depart from the perennial storehouse of classic narratives.

THE FIRST ENCOUNTER WITH THE OLD MAN

Next, the prince must encounter a destructive old man, who at the beginning is still asleep in the castle. The most recent turn of events is enough to rouse him from his slumber. He is introduced to the reader as a man who bought the young princess and confined her to the sewers until she would agree to fulfill his demands. The tale presents us with a revolting image of how he lets her waste away there.

It is no accident that it is an old man who wants to merge with a young woman. If we view the story as dealing with intergenerational issues, we notice that persons from the older generation are making demands after their time has passed. They are not able to relinquish their claims on life, cannot hand its management over to the next generation. No doubt this incapacity stems from having been deprived in some way.

Considering that the prince's father is described as a paragon of virtue, we can assume that the old man portrays a split-off part of the father image, a dark part that the virtuous father did not acknowledge in his life. The hero must confront the father's shadow. The fight with the old man refers to the myth of Oedipus, which we recognize as a subplot, even if the son's conscious efforts are directed at avoiding the rivalry that comes to expression as parricide in the myth.

Psychologically, the old man is an image of maliciousness that is associated with the older generation, and that poses a threat as soon as the shirt is removed, which signals the ability to stand up for one's rights. The old man embodies a will to power, domination, and obedience.

The old man demonstrates this will to power by confining the girl to the sewers as long as she refuses to do what he says. If the feminine element does not comply, it is oppressed. This describes a typical marital dynamic that was common in the previous generation. Women who did not obey their husbands were punished. This explains why the queen's portrayal is so one-dimensional. Her degree of independence places her in a class that is not condoned by society. Everything that we associate with the feminine principle—eros, sexuality, sensuality—has been condemned to the sewers. Pitting himself against this attitude, the prince compels the old man to free the girl.

We met the figure of the old man in Peter's dreams as well, and Peter came to despise the old man in the folktale. In his dream, the man had the strength of an old man as well as a young man. In the terms of the story, he had "put on the white shirt" of the young man. When Peter failed to "put on the shirt," he was being indecisive and bowing unnecessarily to the power of the fathers.

Gradually Peter saw that through his compulsion to "raise women out of the gutter" he had been attempting to correct his father's behavior. Previously, he had viewed what he was doing as compensating for patriarchy. Since patriarchy had put women down into the sewers, it was his job to lift them up again. At this point, he also became more clearly aware than ever of how his father treated women—including his mother—"like shit," and that he had taken on the task of righting the wrongs committed by his father.

When he began to admit how ambivalent he was about his efforts to save women, he realized that the old man was a part of himself as well. On the one hand, he really wanted to help these women, but on the other, he didn't want to give them their freedom after all. Suddenly he was face to face with his own power shadow. He saw how he wanted to help women stand up for their rights, and that this was a task that he had unconsciously assumed on behalf of his mother. But he also saw that he wanted to be able to determine what these "rights" would consist of—in the final analysis, he didn't really think women were capable or deserving of autonomy. He also became aware of how he had projected his own needy qualities onto women. He was learning how to recognize what he himself needed, and how to accept help.

In the language of the folktale, Peter heard the lament of the feminine, and he had a sword that could put the old man in his place for a while, but not for good.

THE FIRST RELATIONSHIP WITH A WOMAN

The folktale portrays forward development. The prince and princess promise to marry each other. For the first time in the tale, a bond is forged of love and affection rather than of power and compulsion.

Given the tale's emphasis on the love story with the princess from the sewers, I interpret the folktale as a search for relationship, and as an illustration of what happens when a young man is strongly bound to his mother such that he is ruled by the principle of having and holding, and suffers from the inability to let others be. Thus I view the girl as an independent person—not an aspect of the prince—someone with whom the prince could have a real relationship. Naturally, it would also be possible to see her as a dynamic and fascinating part of the prince's personality.

By now the prince should be far enough along emotionally to be able to recognize the woman's true inner beauty rather than seeing her as someone to rescue. At the adolescent level of masculine development, there is often a tendency to make girls into something dirty and untouchable if they become too seductive. Unfortunately, this devaluation of and defense against mothers and women does not always end with puberty.

But the princess has captured his heart, and he dreams of marrying her. Their initial encounter does not last for long. Before becoming more deeply involved, she wants to visit home. The prince is so prompt in readying a ship to take her, we wonder if he really wants her back as soon as possible—or did he bite off a little more than he could chew? Maybe he needs the pause. It appears that both are somewhat anxious about committing too deeply too soon.

This turn of events is convenient for the queen, who has plans to destroy both the girl and her son. The mother complex now takes control. The moment there is any hint of forward movement, the negative dimension of the mother complex asserts itself.

THE PRINCESS AS SERVANT

The queen sends the girl away with the sea captain, whom she has bribed, but her plan doesn't work. In desperation the girl turns to God for help and is blessed with an idea of how to save herself.

Turning to the Great Father, she is rescued. Her idea shows that she is counting on her prince to come to her rescue as well.

But first the young woman will be required to take another step in her personal liberation, a step that will not be achieved without first overcoming some resistance. Her idea is to serve others—a quite radical idea for a princess. It makes sense when one considers what kind of people her parents are. Her father subjects himself to the letter of the law, and her mother is frightened of what happens to those who don't keep their word with God. Both are under the rule of a father complex, and a bit naive about real life.

The princess asks nothing for her service except the privilege of witnessing the life stories of those who come her way. She lives like a Mother Theresa, develops maternal qualities, and gathers experience that helps her outgrow her naiveté. She comes directly into contact with life in all of its colors. Psychologically, at the subjective level, she is learning how to take a maternal attitude toward the various needy and homeless parts of herself, to see them, nourish them, and bid them farewell again. She becomes acquainted with many aspects of herself, gets a taste of the many things she could do in life without fixating on any one of them. Of course she will have to develop these maternal qualities further if she is going to be able to enter into a relationship later on.

THE PRINCE WITH THE MOTHER
AND THE OLD MAN

Meanwhile, something atrocious takes place in the castle. The old man and the contemptuous mother make a pact to kill the young man. This would satisfy the mother's greed for revenge, which is shared by the old man, who was humiliated when the prince came and rescued the princess. Unfortunately, this is a classic situation: one step forward, and all the ground that has been gained seems to be forfeited again. He falls prey to the kind of tricks his mother has used all along to keep him back and ruin him.

First she pretends that she is sick and that only the lion cub can cure her. Naturally a loving son will do everything to save his mother. She really is sick, though—sick from the insult that makes her so vengeful and stubborn. But her sickness is a deceit designed to send her son to the lions, which she assumed would be the end of him. However, something else usually comes of such tricks—in life no less than in folktales. Often when we are sent on an errand for someone else, we end up getting something we need for ourselves. In this case, the lion cub is an agent that is healing for both mother and son.

In Egyptian mythology, lions are consorts of the Mother Goddess. They depict her catlike quality, her strength of instinct, and the independence of her nature. Aware of their power and might, lions can afford to act rather casually. They have an untamed and yet sovereign and collected kind of energy. Only in emergencies do they need to demonstrate their power, but they do not hesitate to show it, given good cause. If the mother in our tale were able to tap the sources of this kind of energy within herself, she might be able to let go of her hatred. Indeed, the young man discovers some of this energy in the process of fetching the lion cub.

But the mother cannot accept this potential cure. Instead, she clings to her hatred. However, the good son is not exactly free of his narcissism. He enjoys her exaggerated praise, as if the celebration that she puts on were in recognition of his ability to act independently while still winning his mother's admiration—a classic wish to have one's cake and eat it too. By now the folktale has made clear that the young man is in great danger.

Accompanying every separation—whether from one's parents or from one's parental complexes—we find the perennial stages of the mourning process: following the first step toward separation comes a phase of rapprochement, in which it seems as if the movement toward separation had been annulled, as if things had returned to the status quo. But not long after comes a rapprochement crisis, when everything that called for a separation in the first place becomes reactivated and calls out more desperately than ever for a separation. The rapprochement has the function of painfully reminding one of what was left behind—what was problematic as well as attractive about it. One more good look at both is necessary to get on with the work of mourning that is to follow.[52]

INTO THE LION PIT

Under the impression that the old and new have come together in a phase of renewed cooperation, the prince lets his vigilance slacken. He has fallen asleep, and does not know what the mother and old man have in store for him. They blind him and throw him to the lions. He is naive in the face of evil intentions. Not that the mother has given him any opportunity to see what she was up to. As readers of the tale we are privileged to know how false her love is. One would hope that he would develop an instinct for sensing the falsity of her feelings, but he doesn't yet seem to be able to do this. The prince's naiveté in the face of evil is, after all, part of what comes from an originally positive mother complex. Evil is denied, or is seen only among "them." One is not prepared for anything really bad to hit home. If it does, there is a reaction of profound injury and depression.

The scene in which the prince is blinded has a significant parallel with Peter's dream. Can the folktale help us understand the psychological background of the dream in which he sits blindly in the cat cage? To what extent does Peter fall into the trap of fulfilling his mother's wishes, whose intention is to prevent his steps toward autonomy? Are these the wishes of his real mother, or of the inner mother and maternal presence? And was he denying the threat posed by the old man? These were questions that Peter wrestled with. The dream really seemed to him like a segment of the folktale; he had the feeling that the folktale was about his life. Here he recalled several times in his life when he felt he had "caged" himself, brought himself down, and sought the comfort of women.

What all of these memories had in common was his great fear of disapproval. His need for approval was so great, it didn't even matter if it was sincere.

This attitude can be portrayed as a state of being "blind" and "imprisoned." You are caught and stopped dead in your tracks if you can't look around to see what is happening to you. What has been arrested is the constructive aggression that is expressed in healthy competition, taking action, and setting limits.

In what way did Peter underestimate the danger of the old man? Peter let himself be cut down by authority figures. Overlooking the part that rivalry played, he blindly thought that they wanted what was best for him. He found himself doubting humanity's inherent goodness when he realized that he had been used—or that others intended harm. And he could not bear the thought that all other men were wiser than him. He saw all of his contemporaries as old men, old and compliant before their time. Peter had a serious issue of rivalry that he was not aware of, and did not want to be aware of.

The cats in his dream—like the lions in the story—were comforting and ensured his survival. Natural maternal instincts, symbolized in animal form, became emotionally available. Although these welcome animal instincts were there for him, he did not seem to be able to get out of the rut that he shared with them. The time had come to remove himself from this dangerous position.

The prince seems to have had to suffer a brutal fall from the position of a celebrated son to that of a throw-away cripple. He experiences the wish to die. Once his eyesight has been restored and he sees the evil perpetrated by his mother and the old man, he sees nothing but the dark side of everything. He becomes severely depressed. But his inner life impulse pulls him through, in spite of the catastrophic depths of his disappointment. This is comparable to moments of resignation in which one welcomes one's death, and yet the body lives on, thanks to an inextinguishable inner spark of life.

By feeding from the same meat as the lions, his lion nature

comes forth with a toughness of spirit that outlasts even the most dismal situations. Cats have nine lives, according to the saying. However, his spirit is not only tough but also gentle. He is accepted as one of the cubs—now by an animal rather than a human mother. He regresses to a vital level, which "consoles" him and keeps him alive.

OUT OF THE LION PIT INTO THE LIGHT

The way out of the cage resembles a second birth. The image suggests a decisive transformation of the personality that results in new ways of being in the world. The prince shows that he is behaving in ways he is not accustomed to when he surrenders his protective sheathing and enters the unknown. On the path of adventure and confrontation there are no guarantees that he will have enough to eat or of anything else. Risking his life, he finds it. Here his mother has nothing more to say.

Peter was struck by the folktale's image of exit from the cage. By now his dreams of being caged had ceased. This change augmented his decision to follow the path of the hero of the tale. Stepping out of the cage forced him to take real risks. His depressed mood had not lifted, and the path he now chose meant dispensing with a number of security blankets that he had incorporated into his life. He had only himself to depend on now. What he had to do, he now saw, was go his own way. Never before had he lived on his own and taken care of himself. The first thing this involved was facing directly his "miserable life" without blurring the issue by getting involved in a hundred activities that would tie him down.

Peter wondered if he had to live up to the entire folktale. In part, this justifiable question served to distract him from the tasks that he was facing. But it was also evidence that he could not simply imitate the deeds of the folktale hero—that would be anything but autonomy. This is important when working with folktales. When comparing one's own way through life with the path of the folktale hero, part of the way may seem identical. It is not the point to achieve complete congruence.

Although Peter was voicing doubts about whether the folktale really applied to his situation, he continued to make use of it—now in order to look at his relationships with women.

Returning to the prince's journey, we note that once he has left the cage, we have moved beyond the emotional low point of the tale. By finding a ship and winning the captain's trust, he finds someone to care for him and gains distance from the emotional realm that was so painful. The ship affords him a means of moving to another stage, from where he can continue his journey. The captain is the first masculine figure in the tale who cares for him—and who is in fact quite feminine. He arrives at the doorstep of his bride as a forlorn seeker. She has the freedom to decide whether or not she will recognize him. Until now the two of them have had so few experiences in common that she recognizes him only once she has heard him tell his story. She too is a bit blind. By recognizing him and revealing her own identity, she accepts him again. Now he can trust her. Conscious choice, commitment to the principle of faithfulness on the one hand, the principle of trust on the other, are the new emotional capacities that they have developed.

Peter viewed this scene as a mandate for him to be the one to reveal his confusion and needs. He wanted a woman to be able to accept his moments of depression too, and not only his moments of glory. In short, he wanted to provide a woman with the opportunity to develop her maternal qualities as well. But he did not find this easy. The women that he had raised up out of the gutter had all sooner or later developed maternal qualities. And they had seen his wounds. But he was not at all comfortable with this; he preferred to remain the shining hero and helper.

Peter also resonated to the scene in which the prince regained his eyesight, which is not surprising, considering his dream in which he had been blind.

Although the prince of the story has found his wife, the relationship at this point is more one of survival than of pleasure. They are tolerated by those around them, but not accepted. In fact, they are outsiders, living on the margins of society.

The discontented squires portrayed in the folktale remind us that the story is set in a society in which the emphasis falls on the acquisition and display of wealth. The squires also represent psychological qualities of the prince and his wife—parts of the self that have been modeled according to tradition. Their inner squires look down so disparagingly on the life they are now leading that they can hardly convince themselves it is worth living.

The prince enjoys no position of prominence. He cannot test his strength nor pursue adventure. So he turns to himself. There is something left over from his previous affluence that is still linked to his mother, something that formed a part of his initiatory vision. The prince still has the ring, which gives him access to his inner world and the realm of the crows. The crows' depressive cawing warns him that society poses a threat. A culture of affluence has no place for the kind of relationship that they have entered into, in fact, it will not be tolerated. On the subjective level, he is witness to self-destructive, punitive tendencies that are born out of his disappointment with not being able to pursue wealth. He must abandon this unhappy state. The transition is made easier when he receives notification that things will get better once he has removed himself from this state of dependency. It is actually a blessing when the little castle is blown to bits. Otherwise, the newlyweds might have become comfortable there and lost their sense of adventure. With their castle reduced to rubble, they must go on.

The dew that falls so mysteriously from the sky between the hours of eleven and midnight is like manna from heaven. The healing is the kind of miracle that folktales continually provide to mark the conclusion of a serious trial. The conviction finds expression that what has been torn down can be built back up again. Nature heals, dewdrop by dewdrop, as we are told to trust in prophecies of healing and are instructed in the example of the prince's endurance in collecting the dew. The dew that he collects has a future purpose as well. Restored is not only his sight, but also his foresight. No longer does he expect only good to befall him, but also evil. He prepares himself to survive in the absence of luck.

Now for the first time, man and woman see each other—in the moonlight, in the half-light of unconscious intuition, with the eyes of the soul. Seeing means loving.

Peter found in this part of the story encouragement to be patient and wait until the right moment, to gather nourishment from things that came his way, bit by bit, in the hope that one day he would have the kind of insight that would allow him to recognize a woman with whom he could have a lasting relationship.

DETACHING THE RUBY

The prince's worries are not yet over. He is so fascinated by his wife's ruby that he removes it from her neck. He wants to have it apart from his wife, for himself alone. The ruby emits a magical light; as in the famous *1001 Nights*, it glows with erotic mystery.

When the prince detaches his erotic fantasies from his wife and takes them away from their relationship, a new separation occurs. He is inducted into a company of men, and she wonders if he has simply disappeared with the goods. The issue of material possession comes clearly into focus. The prince becomes linked up with a band of thieves, and he competes with the wizard for possession of the ruby. He lives out the rivalry that is a part of the Oedipus complex. We see how much stronger he has grown since his conflict with the old man, which he had managed so poorly.

Peter wanted to be able to look at all the folktale's images simultaneously. In a way, the prince had been keeping company with the robbers all along. It was only that the riddle had never been posed to him. And as long as the riddle had not been posed, he could see no reason for not enjoying life. He was not in the least aware that it could cost him his life.

The ring offered the prince the chance to work his way out of the house in the forest. Drawing on his originally positive mother complex, the ring gave him access to his intuition and that view of "the big picture" that he needed to solve the riddles. But it wasn't as if a bird simply whispered the answers in his ear; he had to wrack his brain for an entire year before they were ripe in his mind. The messages that these answers contain could be stated more psychologically. For one, life can never be entirely guilt-free—not even for a prince, who knows in his bones what it is like to be a hanged man. Second, there will always be a certain dependence on the king for nourishment and a sense of belonging. Finally, he who steals the ruby in the attempt to make it the exclusive privilege of men empties life of its meaning and punishes himself with death.

THE WOMAN IN THE LION PIT

The woman in his life has by now recognized that he has the soul of a thief. And yet she chooses not to abandon him. But within the confines of the castle she remains blind. And back to the castle they must return, in obedience to the folktale law that it is possible to confront problems only after going on a long journey in the opposite direction. Now it is her turn for depression, it is her turn to go to the lion pit, where she will be visited by something of vital importance to her. Like the prince, she regresses to a physical, sensual, animal level of her being. The urgency of this regression is no surprise, considering how high on her body she wore the ruby, not to mention the fact that she kept it safely tethered and wrapped in a bag.

THE SOLUTION

The prince is now in a position to set things straight. He hires a ship, disguises himself as a sailor, enters the castle through the chimney—a pathway normally reserved for devils and demons—and repossesses the shirt and the sword. (He never lost the ring.)

He has suffered through all of the things that were symbolically prefigured in his vision. Now he takes matters into his own hands, finds his wife, and restores her health. We notice, by the way, that he has returned to his beloved role of the shining helper.

He turns his mother and the old man over to his father, who should take care of a matter that was really his business all along. He submits something to his father that would have been a disgrace if he had dealt with it himself.

The end of the story sees the prince achieving rule over three kingdoms: those of his wife, of his father, and of his shadow. His path of tears outfitted him with tools for life. Governing the realm that came to him through his wife, he decisively resisted the lure of domination by a woman, by his mother, by his mother complex, which would have had him shirk his age-appropriate level of personal autonomy.

What I have described here in terms of complex theory can also be described in terms of social history: Oedipus portrays a fight against matriarchy.[53] It was a custom in certain matriarchal cultures for the hero to overcome his father (the old hero) in order to marry his mother. Oedipus behaved according to this archaic scenario, which is why he was viewed as a criminal by the patriarchal culture in which he lived. Actually, the Oedipus myth itself has more to do with parricide than incest. It is more a matter of power than sex.

The folktale describes the continuing attraction of the old matriarchal cultural form. Without this historical framework, it is difficult to fathom the tale's devaluation of the feminine and the queen's violent hatred. She is responding to dethronement.

In the end the solution to the power struggle is for the man and woman to love each other. But it would be simplistic to overlook the level of the story in which man is dethroning woman and appropriating her erotic mysteries into his own secret fraternity. One might have expected the prince to give the ruby back to his wife. But in this relatively long narrative, nothing is said of any return.

Peter saw no relevance for his situation in the ending of the tale. He did see himself "taking the ruby" again and again, but he thought that once he found the right woman, he would be able to give it back. He criticized the prince for making the problem worse. The conclusion of the story was off the mark for Peter. Nor do we need to force any greater coherence between narrative and biography. When dreams lead to folktales, there is usually one particular point at which they have a lot to say to each other. Peter found many points at which he felt inspired by the folktale, which indicates that its plot spoke quite well to his current situation.

Peter made gains by identifying with the prince. It was a relief to discover that his problems—in comparison with those described in the folktale—were less serious than he had thought. He could orient himself according to what the prince did without having to suffer the same consequences. Work with the folktale gave Peter insight into his problems. Most of all, it solidified his decision to deal with these problems, in spite of his periodic lack of motivation.

By means of a "folktale as transitional object," Peter was able to work himself out of the stagnation that his mother complex had placed him in. An important element of this work was his identification with the folktale hero. Not only did this identification help him cut through his indecisiveness, it also strengthened his resistance to flattery. Depression was no longer something to evade at all costs; it might even be useful to him in some way. Like the prince, he was able to affirm the validity of his most basic physical sensations and needs. In relation to men, he recognized and learned to honor his need to compete. In relation to women, he learned to accept his neediness and realized that women are not always maternal—the moon has many phases. The images of the story inspired many of his own images, which became the subject of photographic explorations.

Following half a year of work on this folktale, Peter decided to let the analysis enter the phase of termination. Work with the folktale—which extended over an unusually long period of time—continued to support his drive toward greater autonomy until the very end of the analysis.

APPENDIX:
MOTHER-SON INCEST IN THE DREAMS
OF A WOMAN

A thirty-eight-year-old woman suffered from various psychosomatic disturbances and a mild chemical dependency. She often felt crippled in the projects that she undertook. She wanted to get more education, but did not go very far in realizing this goal—she would register for courses and then not attend. She often felt confused and dispirited. But she had no problem completing tasks for which she had clear directions. She just wanted somebody to tell her what to do—someone to take responsibility for her. She had been married for eight years and had two children.

She had hoped that her husband could give her direction and motivation, but her hopes were disappointed. At first she thought that he was a very energetic sort of person, but gradually he turned out to be no better than she was, with his insecurity and lack of courage. Often she had the feeling that they blamed each other for not solving each other's problems.

The analysand had two sisters. Her father had left the family when she was thirteen. Her mother couldn't handle so much responsibility. She "did too much and gave too little."

The analysand had two dreams that reminded me again of "The White Shirt, the Heavy Sword, and the Golden Ring."

The first dream:

My mother wants my brother. He too likes the way she looks. I think they are going to sleep with each other. I can't believe it. I try to warn him of the danger; he will stay bound to his mother for the rest of his life. I am enraged. If he is going to do it with anybody, he should do it with me.

Her first comment about the dream: "Strange; I don't have any brothers." After some interviewing, it turned out that the brother in the dream looked like her; he had the same eyes, hair, and type of body. Three years younger than she, he was the kind of man she felt attracted to. The mother in the dream resembled the dreamer's mother, who was fifty years old. The dream struck the analysand as strange and even fascinating, but she couldn't make head or tail of it. After she woke up from the dream, she felt "emptied out" and had a hard time getting herself to do anything beyond the bare necessities.

Two weeks later she had another dream:

One of my old schoolteachers wants to help me with my math. I don't understand. He gives me a very angry look and tells me, "I'll come back when you've thought about it thoroughly."

The dream left her feeling "trapped by that old bastard." She was afraid she could neither solve the problem nor get away from him. "I felt like a real piece of shit."

Then came associations to other authority figures and assignments that she enjoyed completing—as well as assignments that were beyond her. The dream and its associations reminded me of the folktale. I showed it to her. After reading it, she remarked, "I could have used a prince like that."

When I asked her if her husband hadn't been such a prince, she paused for thought. Then she shared with me her wish for a prince with a vision rather than a depression; she had enough depression of her own. Once upon a time he *was* a prince with a vision, but now they seemed to have fallen into a slump they couldn't help each other out of.

The first dream may indicate that her young brother animus was not working the way it might. An animus figure would have the function of creating a bridge between family and people outside of the family. Intrapsychically, the animus has the function of outplacing and reinvesting the energy that has been bound up in the parental complexes.

In her dream, the brother animus's energy remained confined to the sphere of the mother. The masculine energy that should push its way into life was still tied to the mother complex. This image fittingly described her state of mind—her sense of emptiness, frustration, indecision—and it corresponded to her tendency to reach for self-medication.

If a woman's youthful, masculine energy (symbolized by the brother) can neither find nor fight its way to freedom from the mother complex, she will remain crippled by both her mother and father complex. She will remain tied to father, like the woman I have been describing, who felt safe as long as she had the guidance of an authority figure. The second dream emphasizes the ambivalence that her dependence creates. The schoolteacher shames her and makes her play the part of a bad little girl. This reminds us of the old man from the folktale who locks her in the sewers unless she decides to "behave": "I felt like a real piece of shit." Now would have been the time for à prince to come riding up and take her away. But is a prince the only one who can help her? Would he really solve her problem?

Peter had a weakness for just this kind of woman. He could offer her a vision of what life could be once she had been set free. She could soar on the wings of this fantasy. She could hardly live without such an infusion of energy, but no human being can provide it for long. Thus I asked my analysand if she had never thought about trying to play the part of the hero herself. I was hoping to get the idea across that the she might find within herself the quality that she was looking for in others. My suggestion did not appeal to her. Find it in herself? That was exactly what her husband . . .

Here is a perennial issue for women. How many women in this situation ask themselves, "What am I supposed to do?" Putting the question this way runs the risk of laying responsibility on some authority who is expected to provide the answers, or on a hero who sets out on a fantastic journey to rescue her from her dilemma. If such a woman could resist the temptation to call in the hero or "go ask Daddy," her inner resolve would more likely begin to take shape. Or perhaps she would meet someone who was truly inspiring without being heroic or authoritarian. It would be a mistake to expect a steady source of inspiration, but a good dose of it once in a while can be very helpful.

This woman's potential—following the logic of the folktale—lies in developing her own maternal qualities, in learning how to mother herself (as well as others), to discover a maternal relation to life itself, in which things grow of their own accord, independently of achievement.

This woman's work with the folktale consisted of discovering how she had been pressing herself into the mold of what she thought would please the man of her dreams. She had been working on a part of herself that was essential to her development, even if she had long been waiting to meet him "out there."

THE ILL-FATED PRINCESS

On Changing One's Fate

Case Example

A thirty-seven-year-old lawyer in private practice began therapy because she felt she didn't know how to have a relationship.

In the course of the treatment, it was discovered that she was extremely destructive. As soon as something began to grow, she cut it down again. This applied to her therapy as well, which was put to the test. The minute trust was in the air, she was hard at work questioning the therapy and her therapist. It became clear that there was a great fear of intimacy, anxiety about becoming committed to anyone who showed any inclination of abandoning her. This anxiety caused her to end all relationships before they got started.

Of course there was a history to this. Heidi, as I will call her here, had a father who died a mountaineer's death shortly after her birth. Her mother never recovered from this death, after which she became substance-dependent. Heidi could remember when she was small having to go to drugstores to get what her mother needed. Her mother led a strange and turbulent life. Nothing ever lasted for long. This meant that Heidi had to prepare for a change of scene every time her mother entered into a new relationship.

Her mother had a number of different boyfriends. Heidi was shuffled back and forth between her mother and her grandmother, depending on how accepting the boyfriend was of kids. Heidi enjoyed being with her grandmother, in whose sphere she felt stability, order, and warmth. Her grandfather had died before she was born. Heidi would have liked to have stayed permanently with her grandmother, but as soon as each of her mother's relationships ended, she was called back again, since her mother couldn't stand living alone. After a while, Heidi developed a method for coming between her mother and her boyfriends at an early stage of the game, which had the advantage of preventing her periodic deportations. There were several variations on the theme. She could be intrusive, demanding, possessive of the boyfriends, or she could try to seduce them. These tactics almost always succeeded in causing either her mother or the boyfriend to break off the relationship. This is how she succeeded in reaching her goal of staying with her mother. Nevertheless, Heidi's mother was more like her child than her mother, and Heidi took the corresponding responsibility upon herself. In the process, she had to deny a great deal of hate in herself. In her mother she saw a nice woman without a home, who at least did a lot of interesting things, and who was different from other adults. Heidi's mother lived with her until her death, when Heidi was thirty years old.

During her studies, Heidi realized that she was bothered by practically all of the happy couples that she came into contact with, whether they were romantically involved or just friends— even business partners who were doing well together bothered her, and she tried to interfere with them. Her disruptive behavior was compulsive. She had a bizarre talent for pulling couples apart, attracting the attention of one or the other partner, and then dropping him or her again as soon as she had it. She had always seen her behavior as "justified," and did not see any reason for giving it another thought.

Heidi repeated her famous trick by "stealing" a co-worker's boyfriend. The co-worker didn't accuse her of anything, which was a big surprise, but rather came to cry on Heidi's shoulder, to tell her that she had ruined the first relationship she had ever had in which she could really trust someone (the woman was forty). Suddenly Heidi felt really bad and at last asked herself what she was doing. This was the reason she began therapy.

This "game" included feelings of guilt and rage at herself. It didn't take long for Heidi to see that a certain pattern from her childhood was being repeated, and that this game dealt both with her fear of as well as with her desire for an intimate relationship.

After ruining yet another relationship, she came to therapy, sighed, and remarked, "I wish I could trade in my fate for another one." I responded, "You can do that in folktales."

My comment was a response to her wish as much as my sense of hopelessness about the whole matter. Moreover, I felt the need for some symbolic material. I wanted to hear something from her besides tales of wrecked relationships. I told her the story of the unlucky princess, the way I remembered it. Heidi then read it herself and immersed herself in it.

THE STORY[54]

There was once a queen who had three daughters, but she couldn't find a match for them all. She was very upset about this because all the other young women around were getting married. What if her daughters—the daughters of the king—grew old without a man at their side?!

One day a woman visited the castle and begged for alms. When she saw how unhappy the queen looked, she asked her what was wrong, and the queen told her her troubles. The beggar woman gave her the following advice: "Take a good look at your daughters tonight in bed. Tell me tomorrow what position they were sleeping in."

The queen did as she was told. That night she took careful note. The eldest daughter had her hands over her head, the second had her hands folded over her chest, the third had them folded between her knees.

The next day when the beggar woman came, the queen told her what she had observed. Then the beggar woman said, "Listen to what I say, Mrs. Queen. The third daughter, the one with her hands folded between her knees, is the one with the unlucky star. It is her fate that stands in the way of the others."

The queen pondered long after the beggar woman was gone.

"Mother," said the youngest daughter, "I want to tell you something. Don't worry. I heard everything, and I know now that I am the reason my sisters can't find a man to marry. Give me my dowry in gold coins, sew them into the seam of my dress, and let me go."

The queen did not like the idea of letting her go. "Where would you go, my dear little one?" But the daughter didn't hear her mother's question. She got dressed like a nun and was off, after bidding her mother farewell. The minute she passed through the castle gates, two suitors went up the front stairs to call on her sisters.

The unlucky princess traveled on until nighttime, when she came to a village. She knocked on the door of a trader and asked him if she could spend the night in his house. He invited her to come in and led her to a bedroom, but she refused, insisting on staying in the cellar.

That night she was visited by her Woman of Fortune, who made a terrible mess ripping to shreds the cloth that was stored there. The girl told her to stop, but the Woman of Fortune only threatened to tear her up as well.

The next day, when the trader went down to see the nun, he found a huge mess. All of his things were wrecked and strewn across the floor. "Oh, Mrs. Nun," he said. "How could you do this to me? You've ruined me. What shall become of me now?"

"Calm down," she said. She opened up the seam of her skirt and pulled out some coins. "Will that do?" "It'll do, it'll do . . . "

She left that day and continued on her way. She went on and on until night fell again. That night she found lodging in the house of a glassware seller.

It was the same story there. She asked to be allowed to stay in the cellar, and in the night her Moira came and wrecked the place.

The next morning the seller came to check on the nun and saw the disaster. He started to scream and have a fit. But when she stuffed his hands full of coins, he quieted and let her go her way.

The ill-fated girl continued on her journey. At last she arrived at a castle in another land, where she requested a meeting with the queen, so she could ask for a job. The queen was smart enough to see that underneath the habit there was a woman of royal blood, so she asked her if she knew how to do pearl embroidery. She said that she was good with pearls, and so the queen gave her a place to stay. But while the ill-fated girl sat and embroidered, the people in the pictures on the wall jumped off their canvases, stole her pearls, and pestered her continuously.

The queen saw what had happened and felt sorry for the poor girl. The maids of the court often came to the queen to tell her that every night some of the china was broken. They were sure it was the girl that was to blame. "It's not her fault," the queen reprimanded them. "She is a princess and the daughter of a lord, but she has bad luck."

Finally one day the queen said to her, "Listen, darling; I've got something to tell you. Things are never going to get better if you go on like this. Your Fate is behind you every step of the way. What you'll have to do is find a way to get a new Fate for yourself." "But what do I have to do? How can I get a new Fate?"

"That's what I'm going to tell you. You see that big mountain way over there? That's where all the Women of Fortune are. That is their castle, and here is the way you'll have to go: Go on up to the top of that mountain. Find your Woman of Fortune and give her this bread. Then say to her, 'Dear Moira who gave me my Fate: give me a different one.' Don't go away no matter what she does to you. Make sure she keeps the bread in her hands."

The princess did as she was instructed. She took the bread and went down the road and up the steps until she came to the top of the mountain. When she knocked at the garden gate, a beautiful, well-groomed girl opened it and came out. "You're not the one I am looking for," she said to her, and went back in again.

Soon another one came out who was just as attractive. "I don't know you, darling dear," she said, disappearing again.

Another one came, and another and another, but none of them claimed her as their own, until one came to the gate who was all dirty, her hair tangled, and her clothing wrinkled. "What do you want, girl, why did you come here?" she asked the princess. "Go on, beat it. Get out of here. I'm going to kill you."

The ill-fated girl gave her the bread and said to her, "Dear

Moira who gave me my Fate: give me a different one." "Get lost. Go back to your mother and get yourself born again. Lie on her chest and have her sing you to sleep. Then you can come back and I'll give you a different Fate."

The next morning the other Moiras said, "Give that ill-fated girl another Fate. She belongs to you and stumbles about, and yet she is a princess. Give it to her. Give it to her!"

"I can't. She should get out of here." Suddenly she took the bread and threw it at her head. It bounced off and fell to the ground.

The girl picked it up, went to her, and told her, "Take it, my dear Moira, take it and give me a different Fate." But she chased her away and threw stones at her.

Finally the girl's persistence broke through this rigid system of allotted fates. When she handed the bread again to the bad Woman of Fortune, the Moira suddenly changed her mind and said, "All right, give it to me," and grabbed it.

The girl was trembling, afraid that she would throw it away again. But she held on to it and said to the princess, "Listen to what I'm telling you. Take this ball," tossing her a ball of silken thread. "Take good care of it. Don't sell it and don't give it away. If somebody wants it, be sure you don't trade it for anything that doesn't have exactly the same weight. Go on now, and prosper."

The girl took the ball of thread and went back to the queen. Her bad luck was over.

In a neighboring land a queen was getting married. She was having a dress made, but there wasn't enough of the right kind of silk to finish it. The people at the castle were asking all around if anyone knew where to find another piece of that silk. They had heard that in a neighboring kingdom there was a girl who had a ball of silken thread. They visited her and asked her please to come to the queen's palace so they could check to see if her silk matched that of the dress they were making.

When she arrived, they held up the ball of thread to the dress and saw that it was a perfect match. They asked the girl what she wanted for the silk. She said it was not for sale. She would only trade it for something of equal weight. She put it on the scales, and *on the other side they put gold coins, but the scales didn't budge. They kept putting more and more coins on, but nothing happened.*

So the prince stepped onto the scales himself. Then the scales balanced. "It seems that the silk weighs as much as me. If we're going to have the silk, you'll have to have me," said the prince.

And that's what happened. The prince married the princess, they had a great celebration, lived a good life, and we had an even better time.

THERAPEUTIC CONSIDERATIONS

Heidi was captivated by the courage of this princess to change her fate. Who knows—she could have ended up with one that was even worse. Heidi found herself identifying with the protagonist of the story. The unlucky girl made Heidi's fate look mild by comparison. If she could do it, Heidi could do it too. From the folktale's heroine, Heidi gathered the courage she needed to deal with her fate.

This is thus another example of how to use folktales in therapy. Identification with the folktale's protagonist can increase the level of courage to a point where one is more apt to take action in dealing with one's problems. The hero or heroine sets an example. They encourage us to go on, even if we don't take exactly the same road that they take. It's nice to know that there is a road through that rough and dangerous land, just in case we lose our way.

I wanted to understand what effect it had to introduce a folktale into the therapy. And I wanted to understand the folktale.

As indicated, I was looking for a way to shift therapy onto a somewhat symbolic plane, to get the perspective that larger images might provide, and to help us out of the transference-countertransference deadlock that we continually found ourselves in. The story gave us a common language, something to talk about, something that fascinated both of us. It was something in common that didn't need to be dismantled right away. It was a transitional object in two senses of the term: First, work on the folktale made visible the dynamics of our relationship. Second, it allowed the analysand a glimpse into the problems behind the scenes, and provided contact with a layer of the psyche from which motivation to change can come.

Much later on, Heidi confided how important it was when I told her the story, even if I had to paste it together from the bits that I still remembered. She had been making sounds of wanting to break off therapy, to which I responded by telling her the story. To her this seemed like a kind of instinctive maternal response.

WHAT IS GOING ON IN THIS STORY?

The basic theme of the folktale is clear: to be able to change one's fate. The story suggests that fate is not fixed once and for all, but rather something that can be worked on, something that one can pit oneself against. What happened before the onset of this bad luck? And what is the road that leads to the place where it can be exchanged?

The story tells us about a queen with three daughters. There is no mention of a king. The problem is that these princesses can find no mates for themselves. There are no relationships that would guarantee the fertility of the land and the continuity of its people.

The lack of relationship can be seen as the lack of real relationships, or as the lack of inner relationship between masculine and feminine principles. With the feeling of something missing, it is hard to do justice to the business at hand.

Outstaying their appointed time at home, these daughters of the queen have no life of their own. They are unable to take the next step in their growth, to leave their mother. What is at the bottom of this? The beggar woman provides the answer: the youngest daughter is cursed with a bad fortune. There is the indirect suggestion that at her birth inadequate homage was paid to the "Goddesses of

Fortune"—to exponents of the Great Mother. Perhaps they were offered too little salt and bread.

In ancient Greece there was a custom of offering salt and bread to the Fates, the Moiras, at the birth of a child. This was done in the hope that if the gods could share in the enjoyment of human food—a sign of human life—they would be more apt to grant the child a long and prosperous life. The custom was based on the archaic belief that spirits and gods need to be given their place alongside human beings if anything good is to be expected from life. This idea grew out of Greek culture, in which there was the belief that every person had his or her own personal guardian spirit—a personal fate—that needed to be taken into account. The fate, who was called Moira, embodied that portion of fortune that was allotted to each individual. Gradually, the multiplicity of fates was reduced to three: Klotho spins the thread of life, Lachesis takes up the thread of life through all chance events, and Atropos cuts it.[55] The Goddesses of Fate, busy with the thread of life, are historically related to the pre-Hellenic Earth Mother, who was also portrayed as spinning thread.

The queen in the story must have had a warped relationship with the powers of destiny. She must have failed to observe them, underestimating their influence. This would explain why her daughter would have been allotted an unfortunate destiny. It also makes sense of the fact that the beggar woman knows how to find out which daughter has the bad fate, while she herself has no idea, but only worries. Beggars depict parts of us that we have eliminated from our lives, parts that have to beg to be given a place.

Wisdom dwells with the beggar. This queen hasn't any place for the kind of wisdom that is represented here. Her way of functioning pays no homage to the goddess. Banned from the queen's daily regiment, this wisdom seeks asylum with the beggar.

In a Sicilian parallel to this tale, "Bad Luck Child,"[56] poverty is the result of war. This story sketches a relationship between military activity and a fate called Star Woman, who is ecstatic and causes the destructive fury. Perhaps in this Greek folktale, too little attention was given to a mother whose divine qualities could satisfy a child of this world. Maybe it was forgotten that every child is a citizen of two worlds.

The daughter who sleeps all curled up in a fetal position is the one with the bad luck. She is the one whose development has been arrested. Her mother is not a bad mother; she does not wish to get rid of her daughter. "My dear little one," she calls her. Her mother seems to be a bit helpless, however, when it comes to protecting her daughter from her Fate. And she manages to avoid telling her daughter the bad news. The girl spares her mother this upsetting confession. Here is another indication that this mother portrays a psychological problem: she is helpless, or "compliant" as we now put it; she shies from wrestling with reality. This goes along with the idea that she has lost contact with the Woman of Fortune and has become insecure about her feminine identity.

Putting ourselves in the place of the princess, we brace ourselves for a shock as her life takes a nasty turn for the worse. One moment she has all the comforts of home, the next she is out on her own. Not only does she suffer the loneliness of exile; she is burdened with an incredibly difficult existential task without having the slightest idea of where to turn for help. Yet she is calm and composed as she goes down her road. The beggar woman "knew," and the girl seems to "know" as well. She cashes in on her inheritance, taking everything that she can take from her place of origin. She leaves.

Covering herself and retreating from the world, the girl disguises herself as a nun. She has entered on a path into her interior depths through which she will end up becoming herself, rather than finding a man. But first she must find out what her bad fortune is all about. Her unfortunate fate is revealed in the things that her Woman of Fortune does.

The first night, the Woman of Fortune shows up to make a mess out of the cloth dealer's merchandise. The girl tries to stop the

Moira. This guardian spirit and allotted Fate is destructive. The girl tries to wrestle with her Fate but can do nothing to stop her, although she does at least pit herself against her. The very Woman of Fortune who spins the thread of life and the interconnecting web of existence is the same one who pulls it all apart again. We see the bold contrast between what she can do and what she can undo.

Rather than bringing various threads together to make a whole, to create relationships, all the energy that is available is devoted to the project of cutting through the thread of anything that might hold things together and bind single parts into a greater whole. There is even the danger that the Moira will tear apart the girl herself. There is the danger of a psychotic reaction. If it weren't for her ability to pit herself against the destructive Moira, to resist taking personal responsibility for her, she would have run the risk of total annihilation. Here we see what can happen when we are attacked by our own destructiveness. Even if I regard this violence as something that I am not personally responsible for, I may still have to pay for it. This is what the girl in the story does. It is a good thing she is still in possession of her endowment. With the coins, she is able to compensate for what has been destroyed.

She already had enough troubles before the night in the home of the glass dealer; things were bad enough where cloth was involved. Now her bad luck turns to the destruction of glass. Of course, everything that human hands crafted with love and grace will be smashed to bits.

We can imagine that some of the wares that the glass dealer was selling were vessels, which are symbols of the human capacity to receive, preserve, nurture, and transform. The "container" is shattered. The girl cannot hold on to what life offers. It slips through her fingers.

The queen whom she now visits turns out to be a good mother. Until now she had always insisted on sleeping in the cellar, isolating herself from others. With the good will of the understanding queen, she becomes integrated. She is given the task of embroidering with pearls. What she embroiders are images from her life. The shards of her violence are woven into the picture. Embroidery suggests an attempt to integrate the fragility of life into the total picture.

Figures step out of the pictures on the wall. The princess is harassed by the figments of her imagination. Nervous and touchy, she takes everything as a personal affront, even the pictures on the wall. Now she suffers from hallucinations. The rage that until now has been directed outward turns inward, dissolving her ego identity. She experiences herself as in fragments. And she smashes a lot of china. But the queen takes a protective and knowing stance toward her. Rather than being deluded by her present appearance, she recognizes the princess within her. She knows that the girl is not bad in character; she just has bad luck. She is able to separate the girl from her fate. The problem can be looked at and dealt with. But when the violence threatens to escalate, the time has come to do something. And the queen knows what must be done: the princess has to find out who her Fate is, and bring her the bread provided by the queen. She has to ask the Moira in person if she can give her up in exchange for another Fate.

One suspects that the queen is another Woman of Fortune in disguise, a fairy godmother who can undo the curse of the evil fairy. In more psychological language, we could say that the princess portrayed the plight of a young woman who behaves destructively, and suffers from hallucinations and other psychotic reactions. She had to stay for a while in a place where her need to be mothered would be responded to, where her problems as well as her strengths would be recognized. Then she could begin to gain more control over her violence. By looking at her violence within the protective space of the good queen, and by taking a stand against it instead of letting herself be swallowed up by it—she has not yet abandoned her pearl embroidery—she constellates the positive mother archetype. There is an opening now in the fabric of her life for something good to come her way—something without which therapy would be impossible.

It is the bread given to her by the psychically nourishing mother—appearing in the figure of the queen—that the princess must bring to her Moira. Bread is what humankind makes out of grain, out of the gifts of Mother Earth, out of nature. It can be left an open question whether the queen is taking responsibility for the girl by simply giving her the bread ready-made, or whether the bread is a symbol for the nourishing resources that the princess has made available for herself and others through her confrontation with her evil fate. In the final analysis, nothing much can be made of one's experiences that might be nourishing for self and others without the influence of the positive mother archetype. This influence radiates through the maternal attitude of someone with whom one has a deep relationship.

The queen knows of the mountain where the Women of Fortune reside. This is an ancient Greek idea; the gods and goddesses dwell in the mountains, on Olympus. The souls of the dead also dwell at the place where earth and heaven meet. And there, at the top of the mountain, the princess will either undergo a radical transformation, or she will meet with her death. She must go to the very edge of existence. To climb this mountain, she needs every fiber of her strength, the courage that comes only of desperation, and the hope the queen has baked into her bread.

At this point the folktale reassures us. So many beautiful Women of Fortune are paraded before our eyes. We are reminded that many people are blessed with good fortune. ("Beautiful" and "good luck" are synonymous in the language of folktales.) Our princess has to be able to survive a situation far beyond the limits of what most people have to deal with. Her Woman of Fortune is dirty and crooked and threatens to kill her. She is uprooted and dangerous. She is destructive because she has been deprived. She says something that we all say at one time or another: "I wish I could be born again of a different mother." Here is another indication that something went wrong at her birth and entry into the world.

"My good Moira," the girl addresses her—but this plea to the

Woman of Fortune's good side is not yet of any use. In general, this is a useful way of dealing with evil figures in folktales. But the Moira drives her back, pelting her with stones. There can be no doubt that the princess's Fate is sadistic, and has put her in the position of the victim. But she is no longer willing to play this role. She has her mind made up to stand up for herself and demand a new Fate. She stands on the solid ground of her conviction and courage.

Refusing to back down until she has given her Moira what she must in order to receive the better fate that she has earned, she refuses to accept the tyranny of self-destructive thoughts. And she shows her intrapsychic persistence. The specter is driven away by the girl's persistence in showing her nurturing side.

Taking the bread, the Moira has accepted the offering that the princess's mother failed to observe at her birth. Not that all doubts have been banished. The girl is still afraid that this twist of fate will untwist itself again, as anyone is who has gotten free of a destructive power and yet may not yet feel safe enough to take a deep breath. One is afraid that the destructive thing might be getting ready to pounce again the minute we relax. The Moira delivers a ball of silken thread, symbol of a fate that is "normal" in comparison to what she had before, and yet its silkiness shows its preciousness. The goddess of fate seems to have spun it specially for her. That was the end of her bad luck, the story tells us. She has confronted violence and survived.

Leading her to the foreign prince, the ball of thread is the result of her good fortune. Trust in her fate has grown substantially. Affecting both the prince and the princess, it brings them together in the end. The extent to which the fate of the princess is bound to that of the prince—or from a collective perspective, the extent to which the "disturbed" Moira also penetrates the life of men—comes to expression in what seems to be only a minor detail—a bit of string—preventing the prince's marriage. But marriage in folktales is always much more than the observance of a mere norm; it is a union of great promise, without which the continuation of human life and the fertility of nature cannot be assured.

The core of this folktale consists of a confrontation with violence. As soon as this violence has been recognized—especially the wound that underlies it and feeds it—then something can be done about it. The wound has been recognized on two levels, first at the level of the Moira and then at the level of the princess.

THE TALE IN THERAPY

Heidi was very critical of the tale at first, in spite of her fascination with it. She was not satisfied with the story's statement that the princess was no longer disturbed; she felt there should have been a better description of how the bread transformed the Moira. By her skepticism, Heidi was in effect expressing her conviction that the Moira itself—her Moira—needed to be healed. Here she was providing information that was important for her therapy. The goal she had in mind was well taken, for unless her Moira went through a basic reconstruction, she would never be free of her concern that she could easily slip back into her old, destructive ways. In the Sicilian parallel mentioned, the "bad-luck girl" brings bread to her Star Woman no less than three times. On her third visit she also brings clothes, a comb, and other decorative objects. And the bad-luck girl's plea also includes grabbing her, scrubbing her clean, and changing her clothes from head to foot. This changes her once and for all.

Heidi chose to make an image of the violence that was personified in the Moira—as had the heroine of the story—to confront it and to stay with it until it changed. She decided to practice this in fantasy. She chose the method of Active Imagination (see Kast, *Imagination as Space of Freedom*).

The task in this method is to activate inner figures to the point where they take on a life of their own—to let them speak in their own language. This assumes, of course, that we are willing to let

them have a life of their own, which means that our ego consciousness may have very little if any control over them. It is then the job
of the ego complex to try to gain contact with these figures. The
work is supported by the enabling conviction that these figures may
well metamorphose if we are able to reach and speak with them. In
the process, it is not only the inner figure that is transformed, but
also the ego complex, which becomes involved with this newly
emerging and sometimes disturbing part of the personality.

One can begin an Imagination with an image that had a particular impact. In contrast to free-form Imagination, here the folktale
gives fantasy a grid on which to construct one's own fantasy structure. Heidi chose to begin with the scene on top of the mountain.
Envisioning herself on top of the sacred mountain, she couldn't
locate any Moira, and she realized that she hadn't brought any
bread with her. She felt ashamed of herself, and went back down
again. "No bread, nothing to give my Moira . . . " She realized that
as usual, she had been expecting to hop right into something without being properly prepared. So she went back to the scene of the
first night in the cloth dealer's cellar.

Imagination
  Cloth is actually quite fitting. Everything I have woven, the
warp and woof of my life . . . In my nun's habit I feel oddly protected. The Moira cannot touch my naked skin. I wait nervously.
  She bursts in—a dark-haired, wild, dirty woman—and begins
ripping everything apart. It makes me mad. I hit her arm. What a
waste of material! She spins me away. I try pleading with her.
"Please stop." No response. "Stop, you crazy woman!" "You stop
yourself, or I'll rip you apart too."
  I am overwhelmed by sadness. It's hard to talk with her.

Heidi's sadness lasted long after the Imagination had ended. She
felt sad about her own violence, about how stupid it was. And she
was disappointed that the woman in her Imagination had refused to
behave the way she wanted. She was worried that she might be too

much under the influence of the story. Her violence seemed mild in comparison to that of the story. In her next session of Imagination, she wanted to give more room to the violent part of her.

I did not have the impression that she had forced her violent side to conform too much to the story-image of the Moira—which of course can and does happen. I understood her concern as an expression of the blow that her self-esteem had suffered from this confrontation with her violence. Here the story could provide a space to "retreat" to. The wound does not have to go the usual route of creating a major, compensating idealization, which in turn only sets the stage for another disappointment and another dose of salt in the wound. The wound can be dealt with by distancing one-self from the figure in the story who caused such uncertainty. This distancing can also have the effect of seeing the narrative figure more in terms of the corresponding figure of the imagining person's psyche. It can also lead to avoidance of the problem.

In the next session, Heidi said she needed to find a name for this destructive, wild, malicious side of herself. She chose the name "Heidrun" (imagined names have been altered here as well). She attached no particular meaning to this name other than that she had heard it recently and that it appealed to her.

Heidrun was also the name of the mythical Germanic goat that nourished fallen warriors with its milk in Valhalla. This choice of name said a lot. Her description of this "destructive part of herself" revealed that Heidi thought of it not only as destructive, but also as "wild." This wild goat also gave milk to the fallen warriors, behaving in an explicitly nurturing, maternal way for the benefit of those masculine parts that had met their end in the heat of battle. Heidi discovered a connection between her "violent" part—which could also be nurturing—and the male warriors. The goat, even if it was only mythical, gave Heidi permission to be very obstinant.

Once this part of her had a name, it was not long before it began to behave more in the fashion of the analysand's choosing. Heidi worked on this Imagination with great persistence. In the beginning, memories from her life were a large part of this work. She recalled incident after incident of having mercilessly destroyed something in a fit of "ecstatic desperation." She felt especially crushed by the realization that she had destroyed her mother's relationships, which had been so important for her. She understood her actions as a child, which did not prevent her from feeling remorseful about them. In her thoughts she apologized to her mother. She attempted to deal less destructively with both her everyday frustrations and those involved in therapy. She had long been aware that she became destructive whenever she felt injured, something she sensed indirectly by noticing that she was feeling brave and in need of controlling her temper.

Since she had been injured so many times as a child, it didn't take much to make her feel injured as an adult. She tried not to attack herself every time she fell back into her old patterns. She set herself the goal of seeing Heidrun as one aspect of herself that at the same time implied another. She had a very caring side that came to the fore when she was involved with people who were somehow dependent on her. She also tried to gain insight into her constant attempts to disparage therapy and her therapist, to remember that in spite of this she remained in therapy, and thus in dialogue with her problems. It deserves mention that her negative attitude toward therapy grew milder once we began working with folktales.

In the end she made the following observation: the princess in the story had not achieved everything in the direct confrontation with her Moira; her stay with the good queen was also essential. The process of recalling the times that violence had played a role in her life, without forgetting those parts of herself that had not been affected by this violence, could be compared with the nights that the princess spent in the homes of the cloth and glass merchants. The stay with the queen, she added, was something she experienced in therapy. For her, I was someone who understood without judging; I came to her defense when she was threatened by herself, by others, and by her accusing inner figures.

I was very pleased to witness this development into a positive transference. When a relationship is structured by the positive mother archetype, the qualities of the queen that she had ascribed to me could also become qualities she could develop in herself. The projection could be withdrawn. Naturally, one might ask whether her idealization was simply a reverse of her previous negativity. Considering the fact that the therapeutic relationship as a whole was not at all restricted at this phase to an idealizing transference, I believe it is safe to say that the positive mother archetype had become more strongly constellated now than previously.

And yet the question remained: Would Heidi have to busy herself with some sort of figurative pearl embroidery, as the folktale suggests? She was not about to embroider in any real sense, nor to paint. She recalled having once been moved by a wall hanging she had seen in which a former co-worker had depicted her entire biography. The medium of the weaving had especially lent itself to a direct and compelling narrative of her life. We agreed that she would go through her entire life history one more time, attempting to replace accusation with empathy. As she did this, she found that she was able to realize a bit of the good mother in relation to herself. "When I see myself lying to the druggist to get that medicine for my mother, I wish I could take myself by the arm and whisper words of reassurance . . ."

These recollections gave her greater respect for herself and for all of the things that she had survived and realized in her life, in spite of the violence. A memorable comment marked the conclusion of this part of the work: "I have bread, I have made something of my fate, I can nourish, I can go to Moira now."

Bread was not only what she had "made" out of her life. It was the entire trail of tears caused by her violence. It was an understanding—as opposed to acceptance—of her violence. This is what the symbol of "bread" said to her so clearly. Bread meant life, violence meant death. Six months after her first unsuccessful attempt to find Moira on the mountain top, Heidi decided to go and try again.

Imagination

The climb up the mountain is long and hard. I focus exclusively on my encounter with Heidrun. There she is. She is expecting me, looks down on me as I arrive. She is awaiting me so she can humiliate me. I won't let her do that to me. I bring her only bread. I ask her to be less destructive, to change my fate. "Please take my bread; it is more than just bread." She takes it and throws it back at me. What a slap in the face! I would like to throw it right back at her. I have to get control of myself. She is the wild one.

A bird circles overhead. It gives me courage. I hold out the bread once more. She takes it and eats it. She goes inside the mountain.

"Wait," she tells me.

I wait, nervous and full of hope. She returns. She has brushed her hair. She still looks wild, but she is clean, and somehow I like her. She will go with me back into the valley . . .

The Imagination with this female figure went on for months. The malicious Heidrun lost none of her wildness, but her destructive rage gradually metamorphosed into constructive assertiveness.

Crucial to Heidi's experience was the discovery of a source of concentration and centering within this violent energy. She learned that being destructive was often the only way for her to keep herself from fragmenting, and yet that violence did not ensure the survival of her self, since the sense of centering it provided never lasted.

It was not enough for Heidi to become conscious of her wounds, to become aware of how she felt injured by the happiness of others, who triggered her past wounds of feeling excluded, isolated, cut off, and unlucky. She was also continually confronted with the question of how to center herself, to be present to herself in a constructive way, especially in moments when she was hurting. Heidi's Imaginations gave her the opportunity to practice centering herself. They also helped to prepare her for the joys and trials of relationships.

Out of her Moira Heidi created an alter ego who was anything but a figure to imitate and follow along the path to self-actualization. Although it was a figure that may well have portrayed the most energetic part of Heidi's personality, she had to confront it in order to invite what was creative about it into her life and get control over what was destructive. The more integrated this figure became, the greater was her sense of personal responsibility for her violence.

The Woman of Fortune from the story thus metamorphosed into a figure who symbolized human qualities. In the process, she lost her divine attributes, although she did not completely lose her numinosity. This transformation is legitimate and extremely helpful when dealing with folktales in therapy.

Yet Heidi never completely gave up the thought that by working on the Woman of Fortune and on the issue of violence, she was working over the evil fortune that plagued her entire family. She noted that violence had played an important role not only in her mother's life but also in that of her father, and that each member of her immediate family had his own unique version of it. When she looked at her work on violence in this manner, she saw that she was not only doing something for the sake of her own personal pathology, but was also serving the "Woman of Fortune."

CONCLUSION

By means of various examples I have tried to show how folktales can be used in therapy—by working with them, and by working on them. The methods that have been described can be used in working therapeutically with all symbols.

The examples I provided are not particularly unusual; they represent some of the cases that I have dealt with in the course of last year's practice. I chose these particular ones because the individuals involved were willing to allow their material to become public.

After years of working with folktales in therapy, I have found that the right tale at the right time deepens the intensity of the therapeutic process—or lifts it out of stagnation, as the case may be. A folktale that is presented at the wrong time is usually ignored by the analysand, as is a folktale that does not adequately reflect the analysand's most pressing problem and unconscious constellation.

We should not forget that in introducing folktales we always change the tenor of the therapy. The moment analyst and analysand shift their focus to the common language provided by the folktale, their view of each other changes, and so do the roles they play with each other. In most cases this culminates in a phase of separation—and increased autonomy for the analysand.

In therapy, the folktale takes on the function of a "transitional object" as described by Winnicott.[57] Just as a young boy may hold on tight to his stuffed bunny when he feels alone—a symbol of his mother, his feelings for and relationship to her, a means of comfort and a reminder of the reassurance that he can provide himself—so can symbols from folktales function as a transitional object.

"Homework" on folktales can serve as a substitute for the therapist's physical presence. But this is not simply an illusory substitute; it is a discipline based on a reality that undergirds the therapeutic relationship, namely, a sustaining and inspiring ground of being which is made available through the symbol.

Contact with the images of the folktale allows us to experience this reality. One's personal story and tale of woe is mirrored in a lexicon of experiences that has been gathered in the narrative archives of human history. This alters the meaning of an individual's plight.

When transference to the hero or heroine of the folktale takes place, an analysand experiences help that comes either from the text or from an idea associated with a figure from the text, rather than primarily from the analyst. Identification with the folktale's protagonist may well inspire the courage that helps us make up our minds and invest ourselves in creative enterprises. There is a good chance of benefiting from the "archetypally encapsulated hope."

The folktale opens up pathways to freedom[58] and roads that lead to a more creative encounter with life's challenges. These new approaches were a part of most of the examples that were presented in this book.

In the case of the analysand who mentioned "The Brave Little Tailor" in the first session, the folktale functioned in a way that should be distinguished from most of the other tales. Here, work with the folktale amounted to work with the transitional object in a different sense. For him, the intermediary space was a comfort zone. The first phase of therapy consisted of enlarging the comfort zone that his favorite tale provided him, for there were not many other folktales that spoke to his way of seeing and being. Only in a later phase was he able to speak more directly and plainly about his problems.

Something that all of the analysands had in common was an imaginative tailoring of the symbols they discovered in "their" folktales. The folktales' narrative scaffolding aided this handiwork. The folktale offers a safe structure on which to build our own fantasy.

The autonomy that comes from setting up an intermediary space based on the symbolic processes narrated in folktales, the emotional energy and intellectual nourishment brought about by dwelling in it, are in my view essentials for psychotherapy.

NOTES

1. Cf. H. Röllecke, "Zur Biographie der Grimmschen Märchen," in *Grimms Kinder- und Hausmärchen*.
2. V. Propp, *Morphologie des Märchens*.
3. P. Smith, "Stellung des Mythos," in *Mythos ohne Illusion*, pp. 51 f.
4. Examples of Jungian Interpretations:
   M.-L. von Franz, *Shadow and Evil in Fairy Tales*.
   ——, *Problems of the Feminine in Fairy Tales*.
   M. Jacoby, V. Kast, and I. Riedel, *Witches, Ogres, and the Devil's Daughter: Encounters with Evil in Fairy Tales*.
   I. Riedel, *Hans mein Igel: Wie ein abgelehntes Kind sein Glück findet*.
   ——, *Tabu im Märchen: Die Rache der eingesperrten Natur*.
5. E. Bloch, *The Principle of Hope*, p. 164.
6. H. Dieckmann, "Der Ödipuskomplex in der analytischen Psychologie C.G. Jungs," in *Zeitschrift für analytische Psychologie* 15, no. 2 (1984), p. 88 f.
7. V. Kast, *Das Assoziationsexperiment in der therapeutischen Praxis*.
8. "Little Red Cap," in *Grimms' Tales for Young and Old*, no. 26, pp. 98-101.
9. Cf. V. Kast, *Familienkonflikte im Märchen*, pp. 10 f.
10. H. Ritz, *Die Geschichte vom Rotkäppchen: Ursprünge, Analysen, Parodien*.

11. A. Tausch, "Einige Auswirkungen von Märchenverhalten," in *Psychologische Rundschau* (2) 1967, pp. 104-16.

12. W. Scherf, *Lexikon der Zaubermärchen.*

13. C. Perrault, *Complete Fairy Tales.*

14. Ritz, *loc. cit.*

15. Ibid.

16. Cf. V. Kast, *The Nature of Loving: Patterns of Human Relationship.*

17. Cf. R. Ranke-Graves, *The Greek Myths*, pp. 12 ff.

18. B. Bettelheim, *The Uses of Enchantment: The Meaning and Importance of Fairy Tales.*

19. Cf. V. Kast, *Familienkonflikte im Märchen, loc. cit,* and "The Lilting, Leaping Lark," in *Mann und Frau im Märchen.*

20. S. Freud, *Standard Edition,* Vol. XVII: An Infantile Neurosis and Other Works.

21. Cf. E. Neumann, *The Great Mother: An Analysis of the Archetype.*

22. Cf. V. Kast, *Through Emotions fo Maturity: Psychological Readings of Fairy Tales.*

23. R. Ranke-Graves, *loc. cit.,* pp. 89-96.

24. Cf. V. Kast, *Wege zur Autonomie: Märchen psychologisch gedeutet.*

25. Cf. V. Kast, *The Nature of Loving.*

26. Cf. H. Maas, *Der Seelenwolf: Das Böse wandelt sich in positive Kraft. Erfahrungen aus der aktiven Imagination.*

27. Cf. "The Brave Little Tailor," in *Grimms' Tales for the Young and Old,* no. 20, pp. 77-83.

28. I. Fetscher, *Wer hat Dornröschen wachgeküßt? Das Märchen-Verwirrbuch.*

29. See P. Schwarzenau, *Das göttliche Kind.*

30. See V. Kast, *The Nature of Loving.*

31. "Mother Holle," in *Grimms' Tales for the Young and Old,* no. 24, pp. 94-96.
Cf. E. Drewermann and I. Neuhas, *Frau Holle: Grimms Märchen tiefenpsychologisch gedeutet.*

32. "The Naughty Child," in *Grimms' Tales for the Young and Old,* no. 117, pp. 103-04.

33. H. Andersen, "The Snow Queen," in *The Complete Fairy Tales and Stories,* no. 29, pp. 234-62.

34. Cf. V. Kast, *Mann und Frau im Märchen.*

35. Cf. H. Andersen, "The Little Mermaid," *op. cit.*

36. "Snow White," in *Grimms' Tales for the Young and Old,* no. 53, pp. 184-91.
    Cf. T. Seifert, *Snow White: Life Almost Lost.*

37. "Briar Rose (Sleeping Beauty)," in *Grimms' Tales for the Young and Old,* no. 50, pp. 175-78.

38. "Ali Baba und die 40 Räuber," in *Die Erzählungen aus Tausend-undein Nächten.*

39. "The Spirit in the Bottle," in *Grimms' Tales for the Young and Old,* no. 99, pp. 346-49.

40. Cf. V. Kast, *The Nature of Loving.*

41. "Beloved Roland," in *Grimms' Tales for the Young and Old,* no. 56, pp. 198-201.

42. H. Bächthold-Stäubli, ed., *Handwörterbuch des deutschen Aberglaubens.*

43. Cf. V. Kast, *Wege zur Autonomie* and *Through Emotions to Maturity.*

44. Cf. M. Jacoby, V. Kast, and I. Riedel, *Witches, Ogres, and the Devil's Daughter.*

45. Cf. S. Milgram, *Obedience to Authority: An Experimental View.*

46. Cf. V. Kast, *A Time to Mourn: Growing through the Grief Process.*

47. Cf. C. Gilligan, *In a Different Voice: Psychological Theory and Women's Development.*

48. Genesis Cf. 4:1.

49. "The King of the Golden Mountain," in *Grimms' Tales for the Young and Old,* no. 92, pp. 321-25.

50. J. Wolf, "The White Shirt, the Heavy Sword, and the Golden Ring," in *Deutsche Hausmärchen.*

51. E. Bloch, *The Principle of Hope,* pp. 158-62.

52. Cf. V. Kast, *A Time to Mourn.*

53. Cf. H. Dieckmann, *loc. cit.*

54. G. Megas, ed., "The Ill-fated Princess," in *Folktales of Greece*, no. 47, pp. 144-48.

55. H. Hunger, *Lexikon der griechischen und römischen Mythologie*.

56. "Unglückskind," in *Siziliansche Märchen*.

57. D. Winnicott, *Home Is Where We Start From: Essays by a Psychoanalyst*.

58. Cf. V. Kast, *Wege zur Autonomie*.

BIBLIOGRAPHY

Andersen, Hans-Christian. *The Complete Fairy Tales and Stories*. Garden City, N.Y.: Doubleday, 1974.

Bächthold-Stäubli, Hanns, ed. *Handwörterbuch des deutschen Aberglaubens*. Berlin, N.Y.: W. de Gruyter, 1942.

Bettelheim, Bruno. *The Uses of Enchantment: The Meaning and Importance of Fairy Tales*. New York: Vintage Books, 1977.

Bloch, Ernst. *The Principle of Hope*. Cambridge: MIT Press, 1986.

Die Erzählungen aus Tausendundein Nächten. Frankfurt a.M.: Insel Verlag, 1953/1976.

Dieckmann, H. "Der Ödipuskomplex in der analytischen Psychologie C.G. Jungs." In *Zeitschrift für analytische Psychologie* 15, no. 2 (1984): 88 f.

Drewermann, Eugen, and Ingritt Neuhaus. *Frau Holle: Grimms Märchen tiefenpsychologisch gedeutet*. 4th ed. Olten; Walter, 1985.

Fetscher, Iring. *Wer hat Dornröschen wachgeküßt? Das Märchen-Verwirrbuch*. Frankfurt a.M.: Fischer, 1974.

Franz, Marie-Louise von. *Shadow and Evil in Fairy Tales*. Zurich: Spring Publications, 1974.

——. *Problems of the Feminine in Fairy Tales*. Dallas: Spring Publications, 1972.

Freud, Sigmund. *The Standard Edition of the Complete Psychological Works of Sigmund Freud*. London: Hogarth Press, 1955 (v. 1).

Gilligan, Carol. *In a Different Voice: Psychological Theory and Women's Development*. Cambridge: Harvard University Press, 1982.

Graves, Robert. *The Greek Myths*. New York: George Braziller, 1967.

Grimms' Tales for the Young and Old. Garden City, N.Y.: Anchor Press/Doubleday, 1977.

Hunger, H. *Lexikon der griechischen und römischen Mythologie*. Reinbek: Rowohlt, 1981.

Jacoby, Mario, Verena Kast, and Ingrid Riedel. *Witche, Ogres, and the Devil's Daughter: Encounters with Evil in Fairy Tales*. Boston and London: Shambala, 1992.

Kast, Verena. *Through Emotions to Maturity: Psychological Readings of Fairy Tales*. New York: Fromm International, 1994.

——. *A Time to Mourn: Growing through the Grief Process*. Einsiedeln: Daimon, 1988.

——. *The Nature of Loving: Patterns of Human Relationship*. Wilmette, Ill.: Chiron Publications, 1986.

——. *Mann und Frau im Märchen*. 5th ed. Olten: Walter, 1985.

——. *Wege zur Autonomie: Märchen psychologisch gedeutet*. 2nd ed. Olten: Walter, 1985.

——. *Familienkonflikte im Märchen*. Olten: Walter, 1984.

——. *Das Assoziationsexperiment in der therapeutischen Praxis*. Fellbach: Bonz, 1980.

Lévi-Strauss, Claude, Jean-Pierre Vernant, et al. *Mythos ohne Illusion*. Frankfurt a.M.: Suhrkamp, 1984.

Maass, H. *Der Seelenwolf: Das Böse wandelt sich in positive Kraft. Erfahrungen aus der aktiven Imagination*. Olten: Walter, 1984.

Megas, Giorgios A., ed. *Folktales of Greece*. Chicago: University of Chicago Press, 1970.

Milgram, Stanley. *Obedience to Authority: An Experimental View*. New York: Harper & Row, 1974.

Neumann, Erich. *The Great Mother: An Analysis of the Archetype*. Princeton: Princeton University Press, 1970.

Perrault, Charles. *Complete Fairy Tales*. New York: Dodd, Mead, 1973.

Propp, Vladimir Iakovlevich. *Morphologie des Märchens*. Frankfurt a.M.: Suhrkamp, 1975.

Riedel, Ingrid. *Hans mein Igel: Wie ein abgelehntes Kind sein Glück findet*. Stuttgart: Kreuz Verlag, 1984.

——. *Tabu im Märchen: Die Rache der eingesperrten Natur* ("Taboo in Fairy Tales," to be published by Fromm, 1995).

Ritz, Hans. *Die Geschichte vom Rotkäppchen: Ursprünge, Analysen, Parodien*. Göttingen: Muriverlag, 1981.

Röllecke, Heinz. "Zur Biographie der Grimmschen Märchen." In *Grimms Kinder- und Hausmärchen*.

Scherf, Walter. *Lexikon der Zaubermärchen*. Stuttgart: Kröner, 1982.

Schwarzenau, P. *Das göttliche Kind*. Stuttgart: Kreuz Verlag, 1984.

Seifert, Theodor. *Snow White: Life Almost Lost*. Wilmette, Ill.: Chiron Publications, 1986.

Sizilianische Märchen. München: Deutscher Taschenbuch Verlag, 1983.

Tausch, A. "Einige Auswirkungen von Märchenverhalten. In *Psychologische Rundschau* (2) 1967, pp. 104-16.

Winnicott, Donald Woods. *Home Is Where We Start From: Essays by a Psychoanalyst*. New York: Norton 1986.

Wolf, J. W., ed. *Deutsche Hausmärchen*. Hildesheim: Georg Olms-Verlag, 1979.